18th cent Junius,   Anonymous

The Letters of Junius

Stat Nominis Umbra

18th cent Junius,　Anonymous

The Letters of Junius
Stat Nominis Umbra

ISBN/EAN: 9783337145965

Printed in Europe, USA, Canada, Australia, Japan

Cover: Foto ©Thomas Meinert / pixelio.de

More available books at **www.hansebooks.com**

THE LETTERS OF JUNIUS.

STAT NOMINIS UMBRA.

EDINBURGH—1793.

R

CONTENTS.

CONTENTS.

DEDICATION

TO

THE ENGLISH NATION.

I Dedicate *to You a collection of Letters, written by one of Your-selves for the common benefit of us all. They would never have grown to this size without your continued encouragement and applause. To me they originally owe nothing but a healthy, sanguine constitution. Un-der* Your *care they have thriven. To* You *they are indebted for what-ever strength or beauty they possess. When Kings and Ministers are forgotten, when the force and direction of personal satire is no longer understood, and when measures are only felt in their remotest conse-quences, this book will, I believe, be found to contain principles worthy to be transmitted to posterity. When you leave the unimpaired, heredi-tary freehold to Your children, You do but half Your duty. Both li-berty and property are precarious, unless the possessors have sense and spirit enough to defend them. This is not the language of vanity. If I am a vain man, my gratification lies within a narrow circle. I am the the sole depository of my own secret, and it shall perish with me.*

If an honest, and, I may truly affirm, a laborious zeal for the pu-blic service, has given me any weight in Your esteem, let me exhort and conjure You never to suffer an invasion of Your political constitution, however minute the instance may appear, to pass by, without a deter-mined, persevering resistance. One precedent creates another. They soon accumulate, and constitute law. What yesterday was fact, to-day is doctrine. Examples are supposed to justify the most dangerous mea-sures ; and where they do not suit exactly, the defect is supplied by ana-logy. Be assured that the laws, which protect us in our civil rights, grow out of the constitution, and that they must fall or flourish with it.

DEDICATION.

This is not the cause of faction or of party, or of any individual, but the common interest of every man in Britain. Although the King should continue to support his present system of government, the period is not very distant at which you will have the means of redress in your own power. It may be nearer perhaps than any of us expect, and I would warn You to be prepared for it. The King may possibly be advised to dissolve the present parliament a year or two before it expires of course, and precipitate a new election, in hopes of taking the nation by surprise. If such a measure be in agitation, this very caution may defeat or prevent it.

I CANNOT doubt that You will unanimously assert the freedom of election, and vindicate your exclusive right to chuse your representatives. But other questions have been started, on which your determination should be equally clear and unanimous. Let it be impressed upon your minds, let it be instilled into your children, that the liberty of the press is the Palladium of all the civil, political, and religious rights of an Englishman; and that the right of juries to return a general verdict, in all cases whatsoever, is an essential part of our constitution, not to be controuled or limited by the judges, nor in any shape questionable by the Legislature. The power of King, Lords, and Commons, is not an arbitrary power *. They are the trustees, not the owners, of the estate. The fee-simple is in US. They cannot alienate, they cannot waste. When we say that the Legislature is supreme, we mean, that it is the highest power known to the constitution ;— that it is the highest in comparison with the other subordinate powers established by the laws. In this sense, the word supreme *is relative, not absolute. The power of the Legislature is limited, not only by the general*

---

* This positive denial, of an arbitrary power being vested in the Legislature, is not in fact a new doctrine. When the Earl of Lindsey, in the year 1675, brought a bill into the House of Lords, *To prevent the dangers which might arise from persons disaffected to government,* by which an oath and penalty was to be imposed upon the members of both Houses, it was affirmed, in a protest signed by twenty-three lay peers (my Lords the Bishops were not accustomed to protest), " That the privilege of sitting and voting in parliament was an honour they had by birth, and a right so inherent in them, and inseparable from them, *that nothing could take it away,* but what, by the law of the land, must withal take away their lives, and corrupt their blood."—These noble peers (whose names are a reproach to their posterity) have, in this instance, solemnly denied the power of parliament to alter the constitution. Under a particular proposition, they have asserted a general truth, in which every man in England is concerned.

rules of natural justice, and the welfare of the community, but by the forms
and principles of our particular constitution. If this doctrine be not true,
we must admit, that King, Lords, and Commons, have no rule to direct
their resolutions, but merely their own will and pleasure. They might unite
the Legislative and Executive Power in the same hands, and dissolve the
constitution by an act of parliament. But I am persuaded You will not
leave it to the choice of seven hundred persons, notoriously corrupted by the
Crown, whether seven millions of their equals shall be freemen or slaves.
The certainty of forfeiting their own rights, when they sacrifice those of
the nation, is no check to a brutal, degenerate mind. Without insisting upon
the extravagant concession made to Harry the Eighth, there are instances,
in the history of other countries, of a formal, deliberate surrender of the public liberty into the hands of the Sovereign. If England does not share the
same fate, it is because we have better resources than in the virtue of either
house of parliament.

I SAID that the liberty of the press is the Palladium of all your rights,
and that the right of the juries to return a general verdict is part of your
constitution. To preserve the whole system, You must correct your Legislature. With regard to any influence of the constituent over the conduct of the representative, there is little difference between a seat in parliament for seven years and a seat for life. The prospect of your resentment is too remote ; and although the last session of a septennial parliament be usually employed in courting the favour of the people, consider,
that at this rate your representatives have six years for offence, and but
one for atonement. A death-bed repentance seldom reaches to restitution.
If you reflect, that in the changes of administration which have marked
and disgraced the present reign, although your warmest patriots have
in their turn been invested with the lawful and unlawful authority of
the Crown, and though other reliefs or improvements have been held
forth to the people, yet that no one man in office has ever promoted or encouraged a bill for shortening the duration of parliaments, but that (whoever was minister) the opposition to this measure, ever since the septennial

act passed, has been constant and uniform on the part of government.——
You cannot but conclude, without the possibility of a doubt, that long
parliaments are the foundation of the undue influence of the Crown.
This influence answers every purpose of arbitrary power to the Crown,
with an expence and oppression to the people, which would be unnecessary
in an arbitrary government. The best of our ministers find it the easiest
and most compendious mode of conducting the King's affairs; and all
ministers have a general interest in adhering to a system, which of itself
is sufficient to support them in office, without any assistance from personal
virtue, popularity, labour, abilities, or experience. It promises every
gratification to avarice and ambition, and secures impunity. These are
truths unquestionable. If they make no impression, it is because they are
too vulgar and notorious. But the inattention or indifference of the na-
tion has continued too long. You are roused at last to a sense of your dan-
ger. The remedy will soon be in your power. If Junius *lives, You shall*
often be reminded of it. If, when the opportunity presents itself, You
neglect to do your duty to yourselves and to posterity, to God and to your
country, I shall have one consolation left, in common with the meanest
and basest of mankind: Civil liberty may still last the life of

JUNIUS.

PREFACE.

THE encouragement given to a multitude of fpurious, mangled publications of the letters of *Junius*, perfuades me, that a complete edition, corrected and improved by the author, will be favourably received.

THIS edition contains all the letters of *Junius, Philo Junius*, and of *Sir William Draper* and *Mr. Horne* to *Junius*, with their refpective dates, and according to the order in which they appeared in the Public Advertifer. The auxiliary part of *Philo Junius* was indifpenfably neceffary to defend or explain particular paffages in *Junius*, in anfwer to plaufible objections; but the fubordinate character is never guilty of the indecorum of praifing his principal. The fraud was innocent, and I always intended to explain it. The notes will be found not only ufeful, but neceffary. References to facts not generally known, or allufions to the current report or opinion of the day, are in a little time unintelligible. Yet the reader will not find himfelf overloaded with explanations. I was not born to be a commentator, even upon my own works.

IT remains to fay a few words upon the liberty of the prefs. The daring fpirit, by which thefe letters are fuppofed to be diftinguifhed, feems to require that fomething ferious fhould be faid in their defence. I am no lawyer by profeffion, nor do I pretend to be more deeply read than every Englifh gentleman fhould be in the laws of his country. If, therefore, the principles I maintain are truly conftitutional, I fhall not think myfelf anfwered, though I fhould be convicted of a miftake in terms, or of mifapplying the language of the law. I fpeak to the plain underftanding of the people, and appeal to their honeft, liberal conftruction of me.

GOOD men, to whom alone I addrefs myfelf, appear to me to confult their piety as little as their judgment and experience, when they admit the great and effential advantages accruing to fociety from the freedom of the prefs, yet indulge themfelves in peevifh or paffionate exclamations againft the abufes of it. Betraying an unreafonable expectation of benefits pure and entire from any human inftitution, they in effect arraign the goodnefs of Providence, and confefs that they are diffatisfied with the common lot of humanity. In the prefent inftance, they really create to their own minds, or greatly exaggerate, the evil they complain of. The laws of England provide as effectually as any human laws can do, for the protection of the fubject, in his reputation, as well as in his perfon and property. If the characters of private men are infulted or injured, a double remedy is open to them, by *action* and *indictment*. If, through indolence, falfe fhame, or indifference, they will not appeal to the laws of their country, they fail in their duty to fociety, and are unjuft to themfelves. If, from an unwarrantable diftruft of the integrity of juries, they would wifh to obtain juftice by any mode of proceeding

b

more summary than a trial by their peers, I do not scruple to affirm, that they are in effect greater enemies to themselves than to the libeller they prosecute.

WITH regard to strictures upon the characters of men in office, and the measures of government, the case is a little different. A considerable latitude must be allowed in the discussion of public affairs, or the liberty of the press will be of no benefit to society. As the indulgence of private malice and personal slander should be checked and resisted by every legal means, so a constant examination into the characters and conduct of ministers and magistrates should be equally promoted and encouraged. They, who conceive that our newspapers are no restraint upon bad men, or impediment to the execution of bad measures, know nothing of this country. In that state of abandoned servility and prostitution, to which the undue influence of the Crown has reduced the other branches of the Legislature, our ministers and magistrates have in reality little punishment to fear, and few difficulties to contend with, beyond the censure of the press, and the spirit of resistance which it excites among the people. While this censorial power is maintained, to speak in the words of a most ingenious foreigner, both minister and magistrate is compelled, in almost every instance, *to chuse between his duty and his reputation*. A dilemma of this kind perpetually before him, will not indeed work a miracle in his heart, but it will assuredly operate, in some degree, upon his conduct. At all events, these are not times to admit of any relaxation in the little discipline we have left.

BUT it is alleged, that the licentiousness of the press is carried beyond all bounds of decency and truth :—That our excellent ministers are continually exposed to the public hatred or derision :—That, in prosecutions for libels on government, juries are partial to the popular side ;—and that, in the most flagrant cases, a verdict cannot be obtained for the King.—If the premises were admitted, I should deny the conclusion. It is not true, that the temper of the times has in general an undue influence over the conduct of juries. On the contrary, many signal instances may be produced of verdicts returned for the King, when the inclinations of the people led strongly to an undistinguishing opposition to government. Witness the cases of *Mr. Wilkes* and *Mr. Almon.*—In the late prosecutions of the printers of my address to a great personage, the juries were never fairly dealt with.—*Lord Chief Justice Mansfield*, conscious that the paper in question contained no treasonable or libellous matter, and that the severest parts of it, however painful to the King or offensive to his servants, were strictly true, would fain have restricted the jury to the finding of special facts, which, as to *guilty* or *not guilty*, were merely indifferent. This particular motive, combined with his general purpose to contract the power of juries, will account for the charge he delivered in *Woodfall's* trial. He told the jury, in so many words, that they had nothing to determine, except the fact of *printing and publishing*, and whether or no the *blanks* or *innuendos* were properly filled up in the information ;—but that, whether the defendant had committed a *crime*, or not, was no matter of consideration to twelve men, who yet, upon their oaths were, to pronounce their peer *guilty*, or *not guilty*. When we hear such nonsense delivered from the bench, and find it fupported by a laboured train of fophiftry, which a plain underftanding is unable to follow, and which an unlearned jury, however it may fhock their reafon, cannot be fuppofed qualified to refute, can it be wondered that they fhould return a verdict, perplexed, abfurd, or imperfect?—*Lord Mansfield* has not yet explained to the world, why he accepted of a verdict, which the court afterwards fet afide as illegal; and which, as it took no notice of the *innuendos*, did not even correfpond with his own charge. If he had known his duty, he fhould have fent the jury back.—I fpeak advifedly, and am well affured that no lawyer of character in Weftminfter-hall will contradict me. To fhow the falfehood of *Lord Mansfield's* doctrine, it is not neceffary to enter into the merits of the paper which produced the trial. If every line of it were treafon, his charge to the jury would ftill be falfe, abfurd, illegal, and unconftitutional. If I ftated the merits of my letter to *the King*, I *fhould imitate* LORD MANSFIELD, *and* TRAVEL OUT OF THE RECORD*. When *law and reafon* fpeak plainly, we do not want *authority* to direct our underftandings. Yet, for the honour of the profeffion, I am content to oppofe one lawyer to another, efpecially when it happens that the King's Attorney General has virtually difclaimed the doctrine by which the Chief Juftice meant to infure fuccefs to the profecution. The opinion of the plaintiff's counfel (however it may be otherwife infignificant) is weighty in the fcale of the defendant.—*My Lord Chief Juftice De Grey*, who filed the information *ex officio*, is directly with me. If he had concurred in *Lord Mansfield's* doctrine, the trial muft have been a very fhort one. The facts were either admitted by *Woodfall's* counfel, or eafily proved to the fatisfaction of the jury. But *Mr. De Grey*, far from thinking he fhould acquit himfelf of his duty by barely proving the facts, entered largely, and I confefs not without ability, into the demerits of the paper, which he called *a feditious libel*. He dwelt but lightly upon thofe points, which (according to Lord Mansfield) were the only matter of confideration to the jury. The criminal intent, the libellous matter, the pernicious tendency of the paper itfelf, were the topics on which he principally infifted, and of which for more than an hour he tortured his faculties to convince the jury. If he agreed in opinion with *Lord Mansfield*, his difcourfe was impertinent, ridiculous, and unreafonable. But, underftanding the law as I do, what he faid was at leaft confiftent and to the purpofe.

---

* The following quotation from a fpeech delivered by *Lord Chatham* on the eleventh of December 1770, is taken with exactnefs. The reader will find it curious in itfelf, and very fit to be inferted here. " My Lords, The verdict given in Woodfall's trial, was *guilty of printing and publifhing* ONLY; upon which two motions were made in court;—one, in arreft of judgment, by the defendant's counfel, grounded upon the ambiguity of the verdict;—the other, by the counfel for the crown, for a rule upon the defendant, to fhow caufe, why the verdict fhould not be entered up according to the *legal* import of the words. On both motions, a rule was granted, and foon after the matter was argued before the court of King's Bench. The noble judge, when he delivered the opinion of the court upon the verdict, went regularly through the whole of the proceedings at *Nifi Prius*, as well the evidence that had been given, as his own charge to the jury. This proceeding would have been very proper, had a motion been made of either fide for a new trial; becaufe either a verdict given contrary to evidence, or an improper charge by the judge at *Nifi Prius*, is held to be a fufficient ground for granting a new trial. But when a motion is made in arreft of judgment, or for eftablifhing the verdict by entering it up according to the legal import of the words, it muft be on the ground of fomething appearing *on the face of the record*; and the court, in confidering whether the verdict fhall be eftablifhed or not, are fo confined to the *record*, that they cannot take notice of any thing that does not appear on the face of it; in the legal phrafe, they *cannot travel out of the record*. The noble judge did travel out of the record; and I affirm that his difcourfe was *irregular, extrajudicial*, and *unprecedented*. His apparent motive for doing what he knew to be wrong, was, that he might have an opportunity of telling the public *extrajudicially*, that the other three judges concurred in the doctrine laid down in his charge."

If any honeft man fhould ftill be inelined to leave the conftruction of libels to the court, I would intreat him to confider what a dreadful complication of hardfhips he impofes upon his fellow fubjects.—In the firft place, the profecution commences by *information* of an officer of the crown, not by the regular conftitutional mode of *indictment* before a grand jury.—As the fact is ufually admitted, or in general can eafily be proved, the office of the petty jury is nugatory.—The *court* then judges of the nature and extent of the offence, and determines *ad arbitrium* the *quantum* of the punifhment, from a fmall fine to a heavy one, to repeated whipping, to pillory, and unlimited imprifonment. Cutting off ears and nofes *might* ftill be inflicted by a refolute judge; but I will be candid enough to fuppofe that penalties, fo apparently fhocking to humanity, wou'd not be hazarded in thefe times.—In all other criminal profecutions, the jury decides upon the fact and the crime in one word; and the court pronounces a *certain* fentence, which is the fentence of the law, not of the judge. If *Lord Mansfield's* doctrine be received, the jury muft either find a verdict of acquittal, contrary to evidence (which, I can conceive, might be done by very confcientious men, rather than truft a fellow-creature to *Lord Mansfield's* mercy); or they muft leave to the court two offices, never but in this inftance united, of finding guilty, and awarding punifhment.

But, fays this honeft *Lord Chief Juftice*, "If the paper be not criminal, the defendant (though found guilty by his peers) is in no danger, for he may move the court in arreft of judgment."—True, my good Lord, but who is to determine upon the motion? —Is not the court ftill to decide, whether judgment fhall be entered up or not? and is not the defendant this way as effectually deprived of judgment by his peers, as if he were tried in a court of civil law, or in the chambers of the inquifition? It is you, my Lord, who then try the crime, not the jury. As to the probable effect of the motion in arreft of judgment, I fhall only obferve, that no reafonable man would be fo eager to poffefs himfelf of the invidious power of inflicting punifhment, if he were not pre-determined to make ufe of it.

Again:—We are told that judge and jury have a diftinct office;—that the jury is to find the fact, and the judge to deliver the law. *De jure refpondent judices, de facto jurati.* The *dictum* is true, though not in the fenfe given to it by *Lord Mansfield.* The jury are undoubtedly to determine the fact, that is, whether the defendant did or did not commit the crime charged againft him. The judge pronounces the fentence annexed by law to that fact fo found; and if, in the courfe of the trial, any queftion of law arifes, both the counfel and the jury muft, of neceffity, appeal to the judge, and leave it to his decifion. An *exception*, or *plea in bar*, may be allowed by the court; but when iffue is joined, and the jury have received their charge, it is not poffible, in the nature of things, for them to feparate the law from the fact, unlefs they think proper to return a *fpecial* verdict.

PREFACE.

IT has also been alleged, that, although a common jury are sufficient to determine a plain matter of fact, they are not qualified to comprehend the meaning, or to judge of the tendency, of a seditious libel. In answer to this objection (which, if well founded, would prove nothing as to the *strict right* of returning a general verdict), I might safely deny the truth of the assertion. *Englishmen* of that rank, from which juries are usually taken, are not so illiterate as (to serve a particular purpose) they are now represented. Or, admitting the fact, let a special jury be summoned in all cases of difficulty and importance, and the objection is removed. But the truth is, that if a paper, supposed to be a libel upon government, be so obscurely worded, that twelve common men cannot possibly see the seditious meaning and tendency of it, it is in effect no libel. It cannot inflame the minds of the people, nor alienate their affections from government; for they no more understand what it means, than if it were published in a language unknown to them.

UPON the whole matter it appears, to *my* understanding, clear beyond a doubt, that if, in any future prosecution for a seditious libel, the jury should bring in a verdict of acquittal not warranted by the evidence, it will be owing to the false and absurd doctrines laid down by *Lord Mansfield*. Disgusted at the odious artifices made use of by the Judge to mislead and perplex them, guarded against his sophistry, and convinced of the falsehood of his assertions, they may perhaps determine to thwart his detestable purpose, and defeat him at any rate. To *him* at least they will do *substantial justice.*— Whereas, if the whole charge, laid in the information, be fairly and honestly submitted to the jury, there is no reason whatsoever to presume that twelve men, upon their oaths, will not decide impartially between the King and the defendant. The numerous instances, in our state trials, of verdicts recovered for the King, sufficiently refute the false and scandalous imputations thrown by the abettors of *Lord Mansfield* upon the integrity of juries. But even admitting the supposition, that in times of universal discontent, arising from the notorious maladministration of public affairs, a seditious writer should escape punishment, it makes nothing against my general argument. If juries are fallible, to what other tribunal shall we appeal?—If juries cannot safely be trusted, shall we unite the offices of judge and jury, so wisely divided by the constitution, and trust implicitly to *Lord Mansfield?* Are the judges of the Court of King's Bench more likely to be unbiassed and impartial, than twelve yeomen, burgesses or gentlemen, taken indifferently from the county at large?—Or, in short, shall there be *no* decision, until we have instituted a tribunal, from which no possible abuse or inconvenience whatsoever can arise?—If I am not grossly mistaken, these questions carry a decisive answer along with them.

HAVING cleared the freedom of the press from a restraint equally unnecessary and illegal, I return to the use which has been made of it in the present publication.

PREFACE.

NATIONAL reflections, I confess, are not justified in theory, nor upon any general principles. To know how well they are deserved, and how justly they have been applied, we must have the evidence of facts before us. We must be conversant with the *Scots* in private life, and observe their principles of acting to *us*, and to each other ;—the characteristic prudence, the selfish nationality, the indefatigable smile, the persevering assiduity, the everlasting profession of a discreet and moderate resentment.—If the instance were not too important for an experiment, it might not be amiss to confide a little in their integrity.—Without any abstract reasoning upon causes and effects, we shall soon be convinced by *experience*, that the *Scots*, transplanted from their own country, are always a distinct and separate body from the people who receive them. In other settlements, they only love themselves ;—In *England*, they cordially love themselves, and as cordially hate their neighbours. For the remainder of their good qualities, I must appeal to the reader's observation, unless he will accept of *my Lord Barrington's* authority. In a letter to the late *Lord Melcombe*, published by *Mr. Lee*, he expresses himself with a truth and accuracy not very common in his Lordship's lucubrations.—" And Cockburn, *like most of his countrymen*, is as abject to those above him, as he is insolent to those below him."—I am far from meaning to impeach the articles of the union. If the true spirit of those articles were religiously adhered to, we should not see such a multitude of Scotch commoners in the lower-house, as representatives of English boroughs, while not a single Scotch borough is ever represented by an Englishman. We should not see English peerages given to Scotch ladies, or to the elder sons of Scotch peers, and the number of *sixteen* doubled and trebled by a scandalous evasion of the act of union.—If it should ever be thought adviseable to dissolve an act, the violation or observance of which is invariably directed by the advantage and interest of the *Scots*, I shall say very sincerely with Sir Edward Coke, * " When poor England stood alone, and had not the access of another kingdom, and yet had more and as potent enemies as it now hath, yet the King of England prevailed."

SOME opinion may now be expected from me, upon a point of equal delicacy to the writer, and hazard to the printer. When the character of the chief magistrate is in question, more must be understood than may safely be expressed. If it be really a part of our constitution, and not a mere *dictum* of the law, *that the King can do no wrong*, it is not the only instance, in the wisest of human institutions, where theory is at variance with practice. That the sovereign of this country is not amenable to any form of trial known to the laws, is unquestionable. But exemption from punishment is a singular privilege annexed to the royal character, and no way excludes the possibility of deserving it. How long, and to what extent, a King of *England* may be protected by the forms, when he violates the spirit of the constitution, deserves to be considered. A mistake in this matter proved fatal to *Charles* and his son.—For my own part, far

---

* Parliamentary History, V. vii. p. 400.

from thinking that the King can do no wrong, far from fuffering myfelf to be deterred or impofed upon by the language of forms in oppofition to the fubftantial evidence of truth, if it were my misfortune to live under the inaufpicious reign of a prince, whofe whole life was employed in one bafe, contemptible ftruggle with the free fpirit of his people, or in the deteftable endeavour to corrupt their moral principles, I would not fcruple to declare to him,—"Sir, You alone are the author of the greateft wrong to your fubjects and to yourfelf. Inftead of reigning in the hearts of your people, in-ftead of commanding their lives and fortunes through the medium of their affections ; has not the ftrength of the crown, whether influence or prerogative, been uniformly exerted, for eleven years together, to fupport a narrow, pitiful fyftem of government, which defeats itfelf, and anfwers no one purpofe of real power, profit, or perfonal fa-tisfaction to You ? With the greateft unappropriated revenue of any prince in Europe, have we not feen You reduced to fuch vile and fordid diftreffes, as would have conduct-ed any other man to a prifon ? With a great military, and the greateft naval power in the known world, have not foreign nations repeatedly infulted You with impunity ? Is it not notorious that the vaft revenues, extorted from the labour and induftry of your fubjects, and given You to do honour to Yourfelf and to the nation, are diffipated in corrupting their reprefentatives ? Are You a prince of the Houfe of Hanover, and do You exclude all the leading Whig families from your councils ? Do you profefs to go-vern according to law ; and is it confiftent with that profeffion, to impart your confi-dence and affection to thofe men only, who, though now perhaps detached from the defperate caufe of the Pretender, are marked in this country by an hereditary attach-ment to high and arbitrary principles of government ? Are you fo infatuated as to take the fenfe of your people from the reprefentation of minifters, or from the fhouts of a mob, notorioufly hired to furround your coach, or ftationed at a theatre ? And if You are, in reality, that public man, that King, that Magiftrate, which thefe queftions fup-pofe You to be, is it any anfwer to your people, to fay, That among your domeftics You are good-humoured ; that to one lady You are faithful ; that to Your children You are indulgent ?—Sir, the man, who addreffes You in thefe terms is your beft friend. He would willingly hazard his life in defence of your title to the crown ; and, if *power* be your object, would ftill fhow You how poffible it is for a King of England, by the nobleft means, to be the moft abfolute prince in Europe. You have no enemies, Sir, but thofe who perfuade You to aim at power without right, and who think it flattery to tell You that the character of King diffolves the natural relation between guilt and punifhment."

I CANNOT conceive that there is a heart fo callous, or an underftanding fo depraved, as to attend to a difcourfe of this nature, and not to feel the force of it. But where is the man, among thofe who have accefs to the clofet, refolute and honeft enough to deliver it ? The liberty of the prefs is our only refource. It will command an audience, when every honeft man in the kingdom is excluded. This glorious privilege may be a fecurity to the King, as well as a refource to his people. Had there been no ftar-chamber, there would have been no rebellion againft Charles the Firft. The conftant cenfure and admonition of the prefs would have correfted his conduft, prevented a civil war, and faved him from an ignominious death.—I am no friend to the doftrine of precedents exclufive of right; though lawyers often tell us, that whatever has been once done may lawfully be done again.

I SHALL conclude this preface, with a quotation applicable to the fubjeft from a foreign writer *, whofe effay on the Englifh conftitution I beg leave to recommend to the public, as a performance deep, folid, and ingenious.

"IN fhort, whoever confiders what it is that conftitutes the moving principle of what we call great affairs, and the invincible fenfibility of man to the opinion of his fellow-creatures, will not hefitate to affirm, that if it were poffible for the liberty of the prefs, to exift in a defpotic government, and (what is not lefs difficult) for it to exift without changing the conftitution, this liberty of the prefs would alone form a counterpoife to the power of the prince. If, for example, in an empire of the Eaft, a fanftuary could be found, which, rendered refpeftable by the ancient religion of the people, might infure fafety to thofe who fhould bring thither their obfervations of any kind; and that, from thence, printed papers fhould iffue, which, under a certain feal, might be equally refpefted; and which, in their daily appearance, fhould examine and freely difcufs the conduft of the Cadis, the Bafhaws, the Vizir, the Divan, and the Sultan himfelf; that would introduce immediately fome degree of liberty."

* *Monfieur de Lolme.*

THE

LETTERS OF JUNIUS.

LETTER I.

TO THE PRINTER OF THE PUBLIC ADVERTISER.

SIR, *JANUARY* 21. 1769.

THE fubmiffion of a free people to the executive authority of government is no more than a compliance with laws which they themfelves have enacted. While the national honour is firmly maintained
abroad, and while juftice is impartially adminiftered at home, the obe-
dience of the fubject will be voluntary, cheerful, and I might almoft
fay unlimited. A generous nation is grateful even for the preferva-
tion of its rights, and willingly extends the refpect due to the office
of a good prince into an affection for his perfon. Loyalty, in the
heart and underftanding of an Englifhman, is a rational attachment
to the guardian of the laws. Prejudices and paffion have fometimes
carried it to a criminal length ; and, whatever foreigners may imagine, we know that Englifhmen have erred as much in a miftaken
zeal for particular perfons and families, as they ever did in defence
of what they thought moft dear and interefting to themfelves.

D

IT naturally fills us with refentment, to fee fuch a temper infulted and abufed. In reading the hiftory of a free people, whofe rights have been invaded, we are interefted in their caufe. Our own feelings tell us how they ought to have fubmitted, and at what moment it would have been treachery to themfelves not to have refifted. How much warmer will be our refentment, if experience fhould bring the fatal example home to ourfelves !

THE fituation of this country is alarming enough to roufe the attention of every man who pretends to a concern for the public welfare. Appearances juftify fufpicion ; and when the fafety of a nation is at ftake, fufpicion is a juft ground of inquiry. Let us enter into it with candour and decency. Refpect is due to the ftation of minifters ; and, if a refolution muft at laft be taken, there is none fo likely to be fupported with firmnefs as that which has been adopted with moderation.

THE ruin or profperity of a ftate depends fo much upon the adminiftration of its government, that, to be acquainted with the merit of a miniftry, we need only obferve the condition of the people. If we fee them obedient to the laws, profperous in their induftry, united at home, and refpected abroad, we may reafonably prefume that their affairs are conducted by men of experience, abilities, and virtue. If, on the contrary, we fee an univerfal fpirit of diftruft and diffatisfaction, a rapid decay of trade, diffenfions in all parts of the empire, and a total lofs of refpect in the eyes of foreign powers, we may pronounce without hefitation, that the government of that country is weak, diftracted, and corrupt. The multitude, in all countries, are patient to a certain point. Ill-ufage may roufe their indignation, and hurry them into exceffes ; but the original fault is in government. Perhaps there never was an inftance of a change, in the circumftances and temper of a whole nation, fo fudden and extraordinary as that which the mifconduct of minifters has, within thefe few years, produced in Great Britain. When our gracious Sovereign afcended the throne, we were a flourifhing and a contented people. If the perfonal virtues of a king could have infured the happinefs of his fubjects, the fcene could not have altered fo entirely as it has done. The idea of uniting all parties, of trying all characters, and diftributing the offices of ftate by rotation, was gracious and benevolent to an extreme, though it has not yet produced the many falutary effects which were intended by it. To fay nothing of the wifdom of fuch a plan, it undoubtedly arofe from an unbounded goodnefs of heart, in which folly had no fhare. It was not a capricious partiality to new faces ;—it was not a natural turn for low intrigue ;—nor was it the treacherous amufement of double and triple negociations. No, Sir ; it arofe from a continued anxiety, in the pureft of all poffible hearts, for the general welfare. Unfortunately for us, the event has not been anfwerable to the defign. After a rapid fucceffion of changes, we are reduced to that ftate, which hardly any change can mend. Yet there is no extremity of diftrefs, which of itfelf ought to reduce a great nation to defpair. It is not the diforder, but the phyfician ;—it is not a cafual concurrence of calamitous circumftances ;—it is the pernicious hand of government, which alone can make a whole people defperate.

WITHOUT much political fagacity, or any extraordinary depth of obfervation, we need only mark how the principal departments of the ftate are beftowed, and look no farther for the true caufe of every mifchief that befals us.

* THE finances of a nation, finking under its debts and expences, are committed to a young nobleman already ruined by play. Intro-

---

* The Duke of Grafton took the office of Secretary of State, with an engagement to fupport the Marquis of Rockingham's adminiftration. He refigned however in a little time, under pretence that he could not act without Lord Chatham, nor bear to fee Mr Wilkes abandoned; but that under Lord Chatham he would act in any office. This was the fignal of Lord Rockingham's difmiffion. When Lord Chatham came in, the Duke got poffeffion of the Treafury. Reader, mark the confequence.

duced to act under the aufpices of Lord Chatham, and left at the
head of affairs by that nobleman's retreat, he became minifter by accident; but deferting the principles and profeffions which gave him
a moment's popularity, we fee him, from every honourable, engagement to the public, an apoftate by defign. As for bufinefs, the world
yet knows nothing of his talents or refolution ; unlefs a wayward, wa-
vering inconfiftency be a mark of genius, and caprice a demonftra-
tion of fpirit.   It may be faid, perhaps, that it is his Grace's pro-
vince, as furely it is his paffion, rather to diftribute than to fave the
public money ; and that while Lord North is Chancellor of the Exchequer, the Firft Lord of the Treafury may be as thoughtlefs and
extravagant as he pleafes.   I hope, however, he will not rely too
much on the fertility of Lord North's genius for finance.   His
Lordfhip is yet to give us the firft proof of his abilities : It may be
candid to fuppofe that he has hitherto voluntarily concealed his talents ; intending perhaps to aftonifh the world, when we leaft expect it, with a knowledge of trade, a choice of expedients, and a
depth of refources, equal to the neceffities, and far beyond the hopes
of his country.   He muft now exert the whole power of his capacity, if he would wifh us to forget, that, fince he has been in office, no plan has been formed, no fyftem adhered to, nor any one
important meafure adopted for the relief of public credit.   If his
plan for the fervice of the current year be not irrevocably fixed on,
let me warn him to think ferioufly of confequences before he ven-
tures to increafe the public debt.   Outraged and oppreffed as we are,
this nation will not bear, after a fix years peace, to fee new millions
borrowed, without an eventual diminution of debt, or reduction of
intereft.   The attempt might roufe a fpirit of refentment, which
might reach beyond the facrifice of a minifter.   As to the debt upon
the civil lift, the people of England expect that it will not be paid
without a ftrict inquiry how it was incurred.   If it muft be paid by
parliament, let me advife the Chancellor of the Exchequer to think
of fome better expedient than a lottery.   To fupport an expenfive

war, or in circumftances of abfolute neceffity, a lottery may perhaps be allowable; but, befides that it is at all times the very worft way of raifing money upon the people, I think it ill becomes the royal dignity to have the debts of a King provided for, like the repairs of a country bridge, or a decayed hofpital. The management of the King's affairs in the Houfe of Commons cannot be more difgraced than it has been. A leading minifter * repeatedly called down for abfolute ignorance ;—ridiculous motions ridiculoufly withdrawn ;— deliberate plans difconcerted, and a week's preparation of graceful oratory loft in a moment, give us fome though not adequate idea of Lord North's parliamentary abilities and influence. Yet before he had the misfortune of being Chancellor of the Exchequer, he was neither an objeđt of derifion to his enemies, nor of melancholy pity to his friends.

A SERIES of inconfiftent meafures has alienated the colonies from. their duty as fubjeđts, and from their natural affeđtion to their common country. When Mr. Grenville was placed at the head of the Treafury, he felt the impoffibility of Great Britain's fupporting fuch an eftablifhment as her former fuccefles had made indifpenfable, and at the fame time of giving any fenfible relief to foreign trade, and to the weight of the public debt. He thought it equitable that thofe parts of the empire, which had benefited moft by the expences of the war, fhould contribute fomething to the expences of the peace, and he had no doubt of the conftitutional right vefted in parliament to raife the contribution. But, unfortunately for this country, Mr. Grenville was at any rate to be diftreffed becaufe he was minifter; and Mr. Pitt § and Lord Camden were to be the patrons of America, becaufe they were in oppofition. Their declaration gave fpirit and argument to the colonies ; and while perhaps they meant

---

* This happened frequently to poor Lord North. Lord Chatham ! § Yet *Junius* has been called the partizan of

no more than the ruin of a minifter, they in effect divided one half
of the empire from the other.

Under one adminiftration, the ftamp-act is made ; under the fecond, it is repealed ; under the third, in fpite of all experience, a
new mode of taxing the colonies is invented, and a queftion revived which ought to have been buried in oblivion. In thefe circumftances a new office is eftablifhed for the bufinefs of the planta-
tions, and the Earl of Hilfborough called forth, at a moft critical
feafon, to govern America. The choice at leaft announced to us a
man of fuperior capacity and knowledge. Whether he be fo or
not, let his difpatches, as far as they have appeared, let his meafures,
as far as they have operated, determine for him. In the former, we
have feen ftrong affertions without proof, declamation without argument, and violent cenfures without dignity or moderation ; but
neither correctnefs in the compofition, nor judgment in the defign.
As for his meafures, let it be remembered, that he was called upon
to conciliate and unite ; and that, when he entered into office, the
moft refractory of the colonies were ftill difpofed to proceed by the
conftitutional methods of petition and remonftrance. Since that
period they have been driven into exceffes little fhort of rebellion.
Petitions have been hindered from reaching the throne ; and the
continuance of one of the principal affemblies refted upon an arbitrary condition * ;- which, confidering the temper they were in, it
was impoffible they fhould comply with, and which would have
availed nothing as to the general queftion if it had been complied
with. So violent, and I may believe I call it fo unconftitutional,
an exertion of the prerogative, to fay nothing of the weak injudicious terms in which it was conveyed, gives us as humble an opinion of his lordfhip's capacity as it does of his temper and moderation. While we are at peace with other nations, our military force
may perhaps be fpared to fupport the Earl of Hilfborough's mea-

---

* That they fhould retract one of their refolutions, and erafe the entry of it.

fures in América. Whenever that force fhall be neceffarily withdrawn or diminifhed, the difmiffion of fuch a minifter will neither
confole us for his imprudence, nor remove the fettled refentment of
a people, who, complaining of an act of the legiflature, are outraged by an unwarrantable ftretch of prerogative, and, fupporting
their claims by argument, are infulted with declamation.

DRAWING lots would be a prudent and reafonable method of ap--
pointing the officers of ftate, compared to a late difpofition of the
fecretary's office. Lord Rochford was acquainted with the affairs
and temper of the fouthern courts : Lord Weymouth was equally
qualified for either department *. By what unaccountable caprice
has it happened, that the latter, who pretends to no experience whatfoever, is removed to the moft important of the two departments,
and the former by preference placed in an office where his experience
can be of no ufe to him ? Lord Weymouth had diftinguifhed him--
felf in his firft employment by a fpirited if not judicious conduct.
He had animated the civil magiftrate beyond the tone of civil authority, and had directed the operations of the army to more than mi--
litary execution. Recovered from the errors of his youth, from
the diftraction of play, and the bewitching fmiles of Burgundy,
behold him exerting the whole ftrength of his clear, unclouded
faculties, in the fervice of the crown. It was not the heat of midnight exceffes, nor ignorance of the laws, nor the furious fpirit
of the houfe of Bedford : No, Sir, when this refpectable minifter
interpofed his authority between the magiftrate and the people, and
figned the mandate, on which, for aught he knew, the lives of
thoufands depended, he did it from the deliberate motion of his
heart fupported by the beft of his judgment.

IT has lately been a fafhion to pay a compliment to the bravery

* It was pretended that the Earl of Rochford, while ambaffador at France, had quarrelled with the
Duke of Choifeuil; and that therefore he was appointed to the northern department, out of compliment
to the French minifter.

and generofity of the commander in chief *, at the expence of his underftanding. They who love him leaft make no queftion of his courage, while his friends dwell chjefly on the facility of his difpo-fition. Admitting him to be as brave as a total abfence of all feel-ing and reflection can make him, let us fee what fort of merit he derives from the remainder of his character. If it be generofity to accumulate in his own perfon and family a number of lucrative em-ployments ; to provide, at the public expence, for every creature that bears the name of Manners ; and, neglecting the merit and fer-vices of the reft of the army, to heap promotions upon his favou-rites and dependants ; the prefent commander in chief is the moft generous man alive. Nature has been fparing of her gifts to this noble lord ; but where birth and fortune are united, we expect the noble pride and independence of a man of fpirit, not the fervile hu-miliating complaifance of a courtier. As to the goodnefs of his heart, if a proof of it be taken from the facility of never refufing, what conclufion fhall we draw from the indecency of never performing ? And if the difcipline of the army be in any degree preferved, what thanks are due to a man, whofe cares, notorioufly confined to filling up vacancies, have degraded the office of commander in chief into a broker of commiffions ?'

WITH refpect to the navy, I fhall only fay, that this country is fo highly indebted to Sir Edward Hawke, that no expence fhall be fpared to fecure to him an honourable and affluent retreat.

THE pure and impartial adminiftration of juftice is perhaps the firmeft bond to fecure a cheerful fubmiffion of the people, and to engage their affections to government. It is not fufficient that quef-tions of private right or wrong are juftly decided, nor that judges are fuperior to the vilenefs of pecuniary corruptions. Jefferies him-felf, when the court had no intereft, was an upright judge. A court

---

* The late Lord Granby.

of juftice may be fubject to another fort of bias more important and pernicious, as it reaches beyond the intereft of individuals, and affects the whole community. A judge under the influence of government, may be honeft enough in the decifion of private caufes, yet a traitor to the public. When a victim is marked out by the miniftry, this judge will offer himfelf to perform the facrifice. He will not fcruple to proftitute his dignity, and betray the fanctity of his office, whenever an arbitrary point is to be carried for government, or the refentment of a court to be gratified.

THESE principles and proceedings, odious and contemptible as they are, in effect are no lefs injudicious. A wife and generous people are roufed by every appearance of oppreffive unconftitutional meafures, whether thofe meafures are fupported only by the power of government, or mafked under the forms of a court of juftice. Prudence and felf-prefervation will oblige the moft moderate difpofitions to make common caufe, even with a man whofe conduct they cenfure, if they fee him perfecuted in a way which the real fpirit of the laws will not juftify. The facts on which thefe remarks are founded are too notorious to require an application.

THIS, Sir, is the detail. In one view, behold a nation overwhelmed with debt; her revenues wafted; her trade declining; the affections of her colonies alienated; the duty of the magiftrate transferred to the foldiery; a gallant army, which never fought unwillingly but againft their fellow-fubjects, mouldering away for want of the direction of a man of common abilities and fpirit; and in the laft inftance, the adminiftration of juftice become odious and fufpected to the whole body of the people. This deplorable fcene admits of but one addition, that we are governed by counfels, from which a reafonable man can expect no remedy but poifon, no relief but death.

IF, by the immediate interpofition of Providence, it were poffible

E

for us to efcape a crifis fo full of terror and defpair, pofterity will not
believe the hiftory of the prefent times. They will either conclude
that our diftreffes were imaginary, or that we had the good fortune
to be governed by men of acknowledged integrity and wifdom ; they
will not believe it poffible that their anceftors could have furvived or
recovered from fo defperate a condition, while a Duke of Grafton
was prime minifter, a Lord North chancellor of the exchequer, a
Weymouth and a Hillfborough fecretaries of ftate, a Granby commander in chief, and Mansfield chief criminal judge of the kingdom.

JUNIUS.

LETTER II.

TO THE PRINTER OF THE PUBLIC ADVERTISER.

SIR,   *JANUARY* 26. 1769.

THE kingdom fwarms with fuch numbers of felonious robbers of
private character and virtue, that no honeft or good man is fafe ;
efpecially as thefe cowardly bafe affaffins ftab in the dark, without
having the courage to fign their real names to their malevolent and
wicked productions. A writer, who figns himfelf *Junius*, in the Public Advertifer of the 21ft inftant, opens the deplorable fituation of
his country in a very affecting manner ; with a pompous parade of
his candour and decency, he tells us, that we fee diffentions in all
parts of the empire, an univerfal fpirit of diftruft and diffatisfaction,
and a total lofs of refpect towards us in the eyes of foreign powers.
But this writer, with all his boafted candour, has not told us the real
caufe of the evils he fo pathetically enumerates. I fhall take the liberty to explain the caufe for him. Junius and fuch writers as himfelf occafion all the mifchief complained of, by falfely and maliciouf-
ly traducing the beft characters in the kingdom : For, when our deluded people at home, and foreigners abroad, read the poifonous and

inflammatory libels that are daily publifhed with impunity, to vilify thofe who are any way diftinguifhed by their good qualities and eminent virtues; when they find no notice taken of or reply given to thefe flanderous tongues and pens, their conclufion is, that both the minifters and the nation have been fairly defcribed; and they act accordingly. I think it therefore the duty of every good citizen to ftand forth, and endeavour to undeceive the public, when the vileft arts are made ufe of to defame and blacken the brighteft characters among us. An eminent author affirms it to be almoft as criminal to hear a worthy man traduced, without attempting his juftification, as to be the author of the calumny againft him. For my own part, I think it a fort of mifprifion of treafon againft fociety. No man, therefore, who knows Lord Granby can poffibly hear fo good and great a character moft vilely abufed, without a warm and juft indignation againft this Junius, this high-prieft of envy, malice, and all uncharitablenefs, who has endeavoured to facrifice our beloved commander in chief at the altars of his horrid deities. Nor is the injury done to his lordfhip alone, but to the whole nation, which may too foon feel the contempt, and confequently the attacks of our late enemies, if they can be induced to believe that the perfon on whom the fafety of thefe kingdoms fo much depends is unequal to his high ftation, and deftitute of thofe qualities which form a good general. One would have thought that his lordfhip's fervices in the caufe of his country, from the battle of Culloden to his moft glorious conclufion of the late war, might have entitled him to common refpect and decency at leaft; but this uncandid indecent writer has gone fo far as to turn one of the moft amiable men of the age into a ftupid, unfeeling, and fenfelefs being; poffeffed indeed of a perfonal courage, but void of thofe effential qualities which diftinguifh the commander from the common foldier.

A VERY long, uninterrupted, impartial, I will add, a moft difinterefted friendfhip with Lord Granby, gives me the right to affirm,

E 2

that all Junius's affertions are falfe and fcandalous. Lord Granby's courage, though of the brighteft and moft ardent kind, is among the loweft of his numerous good qualities; he was formed to excel in war by nature's liberality to his mind as well as perfon. Educated and inftructed by his moft noble father, and a moft fpirited as well as excellent fcholar, the prefent Bifhop of Bangor, he was trained to the niceft fenfe of honour, and to the trueft and nobleft fort of pride, that of never doing or fuffering a mean action. A fincere love and attachment to his king and country, and to their glory, firft impelled him to the field, where he never gained aught but honour. He impaired, through his bounty, his own fortune; for his bounty, which this writer would in vain depreciate, is founded upon the nobleft of the human affections; it flows from a heart melting to goodnefs from the moft refined humanity. Can a man, who is defcribed as unfeeling and void of reflection, be conftantly employed in feeking proper objects on whom to exercife thofe glorious virtues of compaffion and generofity? The diftreffed officer, the foldier, the widow, the orphan, and a long lift befides, know that vanity has no fhare in his frequent donations; he gives, becaufe he feels their diftreffes. Nor has he ever been rapacious with one hand to be bountiful with the other; yet this uncandid Junius would infinuate, that the dignity of the commander in chief is depraved into the bafe office of commiffion broker; that is, Lord Granby bargains for the fale of commiffions; for it muft have this meaning, if it has any at all. But where is the man living who can juftly charge his lordfhip with fuch mean practices? Why does not Junius produce him? Junius knows that he has no other means of wounding this hero than from fome miffile weapon, fhot from an obfcure corner: He feeks, as all defamatory writers do,

———fpargere voces
In vulgum ambiguas———

to raife a fufpicion in the minds of the people. But I hope that my countrymen will be no longer impofed upon by artful and defigning men, or by wretches, who, bankrupts in bufinefs, in fame, and in

fortune, mean nothing more than to involve this country in the same
common ruin with themselves. Hence it is, that they are conftantly aiming their dark and too often fatal weapons againft thofe who
ftand forth as the bulwark of our national fafety. Lord Granby was
too confpicuous a mark not to be their object. He is next attacked
for being unfaithful to his promifes and engagements : Where are
Junius's proofs ? Although I could give fome inftances where a breach
of promife would be a virtue, efpecially in the cafe of thofe who
would pervert the open unfufpecting moments of convivial mirth,
into fly infidious applications for preferment or party-fyftems, and
would endeavour to furprife a good man, who cannot bear to fee
any one leave him diffatisfied, into unguarded promifes. Lord Granby's attention to his own family and relations is called felfifh. Had
he not attended to them, when fair and juft opportunities prefented
themfelves, I fhould have thought him unfeeling, and void of reflection indeed. How are any man's friends or relations to be provided
for, but from the influence and protection of the patron ? It is unfair
to fuppofe that Lord Granby's friends have not as much merit as the
friends of any other great man : If he is generous at the public expence, as Junius invidioufly calls it, the public is at no more expence
for his lordfhip's friends than it would be if any other fet of men
poffeffed thofe offices. The charge is ridiculous !

THE laft charge againft Lord Granby is of a moft ferious and
alarming nature indeed. Junius afferts, that the army is mouldering
away for want of the direction of a man of common abilities and fpirit. The prefent condition of the army gives the directeft lie to his
affertions. It was never upon a more refpectable footing with regard
to difcipline, and all the effentials that can form good foldiers. Lord
Ligonier delivered a firm and noble palladium of our fafeties into
Lord Granby's hands, who has kept it in the fame good order in
which he received it. The ftricteft care has been taken to fill up the
vacant commiffions with fuch gentlemen as have the glory of their

anceftors to fupport, as well as their own, and are doubly bound to the caufe of their king and country, from motives of private proper- ty as well as public fpirit. The adjutant-general, who has the imme- diate care of the troops after Lord Granby, is an officer that would do great honour to any fervice in Europe, for his correct arrange- ments, good fenfe, and difcernment upon all occafions—and for a punctuality and precifion which give the moft entire fatisfaction to all who are obliged to confult him. The reviewing generals, who in- fpect the army twice a-year, have been felected with the greateft care, and have anfwered the important truft repofed in them in the moft laudable manner. Their reports of the condition of the army are much more to be credited than thofe of Junius, whom I do advife to atone for his fhameful afperfions, by afking pardon of Lord Gran- by, and the whole kingdom, whom he has offended by his abominable fcandals. In fhort, to turn Junius's own battery againft him, I muft affert, in his own words, " That he has given ftrong affertions with- out proof, declamation without argument, and violent cenfures with- out dignity or moderation."

WILLIAM DRAPER.

LETTER III.

TO SIR WILLIAM DRAPER, KNIGHT OF THE BATH.

SIR,   *FEBRUARY* 7. 1769.

YOUR defence of Lord Granby does honour to the goodnefs of your heart. You feel, as you ought to do, for the reputation of your friend, and you exprefs yourfelf in the warmeft language of your paffions. In any other caufe, I doubt not, you would have cautiouf- ly weighed the confequences of committing your name to the licen- tious difcourfes and malignant opinions of the world. But here, I presume, you thought it would be a breach of friendship to lose one moment in consulting your understanding, as if an appeal to the public were no more than a military *coup de main*, where a brave man has no rules to follow but the dictates of his courage. Touched with your generosity, I freely forgive the excesses into which it has led you; and, far from resenting those terms of reproach, which, considering that you are an advocate for decorum, you have heaped upon me rather too liberally, I place them to the account of an honest unreflecting indignation, in which your cooler judgment and natural politeness had no concern. I approve of the spirit with which you have given your name to the public; and, if it were a proof of any thing but spirit, I should have thought myself bound to follow your example. I should have hoped that even *my* name might have carried some authority with it, if I had not seen how very little weight or consideration a printed paper receives even from the respectable signature of Sir William Draper.

You begin with a general assertion, that writers, such as I am, are the real cause of all the public evils we complain of. And do you really think, Sir William, that the licentious pen of a political writer is able to produce such important effects? A little calm reflection might have shown you, that national calamities do not arise from the description, but from the real character and conduct, of ministers. To have supported your assertion, you should have proved that the present ministry are unquestionably the *best and brightest* characters of the kingdom; and that, if the affections of the colonies have been alienated, if Corsica has been shamefully abandoned, if commerce languishes, if public credit is threatened with a new debt, and your own Manilla ransom most dishonourably given up, it has all been owing to the malice of political writers, who will not suffer the best and brightest characters (meaning still the present ministry) to take a single right step for the honour or interest of the nation. But it seems you were a little tender of coming to particulars. Your conscience infinuated to you, that it would be prudent to leave the characters of Grafton, North, Hillfborough, Weymouth, and Mansfield, to fhift for themfelves; and truly, Sir William, the part you *have* undertaken is at leaft as much as you are equal to.

WITHOUT difputing Lord Granby's courage, we are yet to learn in what articles of military knowledge nature has been fo very liberal to his mind. If you have ferved with him, you ought to have pointed out fome inftances of able difpofition and well-concerted enterprize, which might fairly be attributed to his capacity as a general. It is you, Sir William, who make your friend appear aukward and ridiculous, by giving him a laced fuit of tawdry qualifications, which nature never intended him to wear.

You fay, he has acquired nothing but honour in the field. Is the Ordnance nothing? Are the Blues nothing? Is the command of the army, with all the patronage annexed to it, nothing? Where he got thefe *nothings* I know not; but you at leaft ought to have told us where he deferved them.

As to his bounty, compaffion, &c. it would have been but little to the purpofe though you had proved all that you have afferted. I meddle with nothing but his character as commander in chief; and, though I acquit him of the bafenefs of felling commiffions, I ftill affert, that his military cares have never extended beyond the difpofal of vacancies; and I am juftified by the complaints of the whole army, when I fay, that, in this diftribution, he confults nothing but parliamentary intereft, or the gratification of his immediate dependents. As to his fervile fubmiffion to the reigning miniftry, let me afk, whether he did not defert the caufe of the whole army when he fuffered Sir Jeffery Amherft to be facrificed, and what fhare he had in recalling that officer to the fervice? Did he not betray the juft intereft of the army, in permitting Lord Percy to have a regiment? and does he not at this moment give up all character and dignity as a gentleman, in receding from his own repeated declarations in favour of Mr Wilkes?

In the two next articles I think we are agreed. You candidly admit, that he often makes fuch promifes as it is a virtue in him to violate, and that no man is more affiduous to provide for his relations at the public expence. I did not urge the laſt as an abfolute vice in his difpofition, but to prove that a *careleſs difintereſted ſpirit* is no part of his character; and as to the other, I defire it may be remembered, that I never defcended to the indecency of inquiring into his *convivial hours*. It is you, Sir William Draper, who have taken care to reprefent your friend in the character of a drunken landlord, who deals out his promifes as liberally as his liquor, and will fuffer no man to leave his table either forrowful or fober. None but an intimate friend, who muſt frequently have feen him in thefe unhappy difgraceful moments, could have defcribed him fo well.

The laſt charge, of the negleƈt of the army, is indeed the moſt material of all. I am forry to tell you, Sir William, that, in this article, your firſt faƈt is falfe; and as there is nothing more painful to me than to give a direƈt contradiƈtion to a gentleman of your appearance, I could wifh, that, in your future publications, you would pay a greater attention to the truth of your premifes, before you fuffer your genius to hurry you to a conclufion. Lord Ligonier *did not* deliver the army (which you, in claffical language, are pleafed to call a palladium) into Lord Granby's hands. It was taken from him much againſt his inclination, fome two or three years before Lord Granby was commander in chief. As to the ſtate of the army, I ſhould be glad to know where you have received your intelligence: Was it in the rooms at Bath, or at your retreat at Clifton? The reports of reviewing generals comprehend only a few regiments in England, which, as they are immediately under the royal infpeƈtion, are per-

F

haps in fome tolerable order: But, do you know any thing of the
troops in the Weft Indies, the Mediterranean, and North America,
to fay nothing of a whole army abfolutely ruined in Ireland? Inquire
a little into facts, Sir William, before you publifh your next panegyric upon Lord Granby; and, believe me, you will find there is a
fault at head-quarters, which even the acknowledged care and abilities of the adjutant-general cannot correct.

PERMIT me now, Sir William, to addrefs myfelf perfonally to
you, by way of thanks for the honour of your correfpondence. You
are by no means undeferving of notice; and it may be of confequence
even to Lord Granby, to have it determined, whether or no the man
who has praifed him fo lavifhly be himfelf deferving of praife. When
you returned to Europe, you zealoufly undertook the caufe of that
gallant army, by whofe bravery at Manilla your own fortune had
been eftablifhed: You complained, you threatened, you even appealed to the public in print. By what accident did it happen, that, in
the midft of all this buftle, and all thefe clamours for juftice to your
injured troops, the name of the Manilla ranfom was fuddenly buried
in a profound, and, fince that time, an uninterrupted filence? Did
the miniftry fuggeft any motives to you, ftrong enough to tempt a
man of honour to defert and betray the caufe of his fellow-foldiers?
Was it that blufhing ribbon, which is now the perpetual ornament
of your perfon? Or was it that regiment, which you afterwards (a
thing unprecedented among foldiers) fold to Colonel Gifborne? Or
was it that government, the full pay of which you are contented to
hold, with the half-pay of an Irifh colonel? And do you now, after
a retreat not very like that of Scipio, prefume to intrude yourfelf, un-
thought-of, uncalled-for, upon the patience of the public? Are your
flatteries of the commander in chief directed to another regiment,
which you may again difpofe of on the fame honourable terms? We
know your prudence, Sir William, and I fhould be forry to ftop your
preferment.

                                              JUNIUS.

LETTER IV.

TO JUNIUS.

SIR,   *FEBRUARY* 17. 1769.

I RECEIVED Junius's favour laſt night: He is determined to keep his advantage by the help of his maſk ; it is an excellent protection ; it has ſaved many a man from an untimely end. But whenever he will be honeſt enough to lay it aſide, avow himſelf, and produce the face which has ſo long lurked behind it, the world will be able to judge of his motives for writing ſuch infamous invectives. His real name will diſcover his freedom and independency, or his ſervility to a faction. Diſappointed ambition, reſentment for defeated hopes, and deſire of revenge, aſſume but too often the appearance of public ſpirit ; but be his deſigns wicked or charitable, Junius ſhould learn, that it is poſſible to condemn meaſures, without a barbarous and criminal outrage againſt men. Junius delights to mangle carcaſes with a hatchet ; his language and inſtrument have a great connection with Claremarket, and, to do him juſtice, he handles his weapon moſt admirably. One would imagine he had been taught to throw it by the ſavages of America. It is therefore high time for me to ſtep in once more to ſhield my friend from this mercileſs weapon, although I may be wounded in the attempt. But I muſt firſt aſk Junius, by what forced analogy and conſtruction the moments of convivial mirth are made to ſignify indecency, a violation of engagements, a drunken landlord, and a deſire that every one in company ſhould be drunk likewiſe ? He muſt have culled all the flowers of St Giles's and Billingſgate to have produced ſuch a piece of oratory. Here the hatchet deſcends with tenfold vengeance ; but, alas ! it hurts no one but its maſter ! For Junius muſt not think to put words into my mouth, that ſeem too foul even for his own.

F 2

My friend's political engagements I know not ; fo cannot pretend
to explain them, or affert their confiftency. I know not whether Junius be confiderable enough to belong to any party : If he fhould be
fo, can he affirm that he has always adhered to one fet of men and
meafures ? Is he fure that he has never fided with thofe whom he
was firft hired to abufe ? Has he never abufed thofe he was hired to
praife ? To fay the truth, moft mens politics fit much too loofely
about them. But as my friend's military character was the chief ob--
ject that engaged me in this controverfy, to that I fhall return.

JUNIUS afks what inftances my friend has given of his military
fkill and capacity as a general ? When and where he gained his honour ? When he deferved his emoluments ? The united voice of the
army which ferved under him, the glorious teftimony of Prince Fer-
dinand, and of vanquifhed enemies, all Germany will tell him. Junius repeats the complaints of the army againft parliamentary influence. I love the army too well, not to wifh that fuch influence were
lefs. Let Junius point out the time when it has not prevailed. It
was of the leaft force in the time of that great man, the late Duke
of Cumberland, who, as a prince of the blood, was able as well
as willing to ftem a torrent which would have overborne any private fubject. In time of war this influence is fmall. In peace, when
difcontent and faction have the fureft means to operate, efpecially in
this country, and when from a fcarcity of public fpirit the wheels of
government are rarely moved but by the power and force of obligations, its weight is always too great ; yet, if this influence at prefent
has done no greater harm than the placing Earl Percy at the head of
a regiment, I do not think that either the rights or beft interefts of
the army are facrificed and betrayed, or the nation undone. Let me
afk Junius, if he knows any one nobleman in the army who has
had a regiment by feniority ? I feel myfelf happy in feeing young
noblemen of illuftrious name and great property come among us.
They are an additional fecurity to the kingdom from foreign or do-

meſtic ſlavery. Junius needs not be told, that, ſhould the time ever come, when this nation is to be defended only by thoſe who have nothing more to loſe than their arms and their pay, its danger will be great indeed. A happy mixture of men of quality with ſoldiers of fortune is always to be wiſhed for. But the main point is ſtill to be contended for, I mean the diſcipline and condition of the army; and I muſt ſtill maintain, though contradicted by Junius, that it was never upon a more reſpectable footing, as to all the eſſentials that can form good ſoldiers, than it is at preſent. Junius is forced to allow, that our army at home may be in ſome tolerable order; yet how kindly does he invite our late enemies to the invaſion of Ireland, by aſſuring them that the army in that kingdom is totally ruined! (The colonels of that army are much obliged to him.) I have too great an opinion of the military talents of the lord lieutenant, and of all their diligence and capacity, to believe it. If from ſome ſtrange unaccountable fatality, the people of that kingdom cannot be induced to conſult their own ſecurity by ſuch an effectual augmentation as may enable the troops there to act with power and energy, is the commander in chief here to blame? or is he to blame, becauſe the troops in the Mediterranean, in the Weſt Indies, in America, labour under great difficulties from the ſcarcity of men, which is but too viſible all over theſe kingdoms? Many of our forces are in climates unfavourable to Britiſh conſtitutions; their loſs is in proportion. Britain muſt recruit all theſe regiments from her own emaciated boſom, or, more precariouſly, by Catholics from Ireland. We are likewiſe ſubject to the fatal drains to the Eaſt Indies, to Senegal, and the alarming emigrations of our people to other countries. Such depopulation can only be repaired by a long peace, or by ſome ſenſible bill of naturalization.

I MUST now take the liberty to talk to Junius on my own account. He is pleaſed to tell me that he addreſſes himſelf to me *perſonally;* I ſhall be glad to ſee him. It is his *imperſonality* that I complain of, and his invifible attacks ; for his dagger in the air is only to be regarded becaufe one cannot fee the hand which holds it ; but had it not wounded other people more deeply than myfelf, I fhould not have obtruded myfelf at all on the patience of the public.

MARK how a plain tale fhall put him down, and transfufe the blufh of my ribbon into his own cheeks. Junius tells me, that, at my return, I zealoufly undertook the caufe of the gallant army by whofe bravery at Manilla my own fortunes were eftablifhed ; that I complained, that I even appealed to the public. I did fo ; I glory in having done fo, as I had an undoubted right to vindicate my own character attacked by a Spanifh memorial, and to affert the rights of my brave companions. I glory likewife, that I have never taken up my pen but to vindicate the injured.· Junius afks by what accident did it happen, that, in the midft of all this buftle, and all the cla-mours for juftice to the injured troops, the Manilla ranfom was fud-denly buried in a profound, and, fince that time, an uninterrupted filence ? I will explain the caufe to the public. The feveral minifters who have been employed fince that time have been very defirous to do juftice from two moft laudable motives, a ftrong inclination to affift injured bravery, and to acquire a well deferved popularity to themfelves. Their efforts have been in vain. Some were ingenuous enough to own, that they could not think of involving this diftreffed nation into another war for our private concerns. In fhort, our rights for the prefent are facrificed to national convenience ; and I muft confefs, that, although I may lofe five and twenty thoufand pounds by their acquiefcence to this breach of faith in the Spaniards, I think they are in the right to temporize, confidering the critical fituation of this country, convulfed in every part by poifon infufed by ano-nymous, wicked, and incendiary writers. Lord Shelburne will do me the juftice to own, that, in September laft, I waited upon him with a joint memorial from the admiral Sir S. Cornifh and myfelf, in behalf of our injured companions. His lordfhip was as frank upon the oc-

cafion as other fecretaries had been before him. He did not deceive
us by giving any immediate hopes of relief.

JUNIUS would bafely infinuate, that my filence may have been
purchafed by my government, by my *blufhing* ribbon, by my regiment, by the fale of that regiment, and by half-pay as an Irifh colonel.

HIS Majefty was pleafed to give me my government for my fervice at Madras. I had my firft regiment in 1757. Upon my return
from Manilla, his Majefty, by Lord Egremont, informed me that I
fhould have the firft vacant red ribbon, as a reward for many fervices
in an enterprize which I had planned as well as executed. The
Duke of Bedford and Mr. Grenville confirmed thofe affurances many
months before the Spaniards had protefted the ranfom bills. To accommodate Lord Clive, then going upon a moft important fervice
to Bengal, I waved my claim to the vacancy which then happened.
As there was no other vacancy until the Duke of Grafton and Lord
Rockingham were joint minifters, I was then honoured with the order: And it is furely no fmall honour to me, that, in fuch a fucceffion of minifters, they were all pleafed to think that I had deferved
it; in my favour they were all united. Upon the reduction of the
79th regiment, which had ferved fo glorioufly in the Eaft Indies, his
Majefty, unfolicited by me, gave me the 16th regiment of foot as an
equivalent. My motives for retiring afterwards are foreign to the
purpofe; let it fuffice, that his Majefty was pleafed to approve of
them; they are fuch as no man can think indecent, who knows the
fhocks that repeated viciffitudes of heat and cold, of dangerous and
fickly climates, will give to the beft conftitutions in a pretty long
courfe of fervice. I refigned my regiment to Colonel Gifborne, a very
good officer, for his half-pay, L.200 Irifh annuity; fo that, according to Junius, I have been bribed to fay nothing more of the Manilla ranfom, and facrifice thofe brave men, by the ftrange avarice of

accepting three hundred and eighty pounds per annum, and giving
up eight hundred! If this be bribery, it is not the bribery of thefe
times. As to my flattery, thofe who know me will judge of it. By
the afperity of Junius's ftyle, I cannot indeed call him a flatterer, unlefs he be as a cynick or a maftiff; if he wags his tail, he will ftill
growl, and long to bite. The public will now judge of the credit
that ought to be given to Junius's writings, from the falfities that he
has infinuated with refpeÆ to myfelf.

WILLIAM DRAPER.

LETTER V.

TO SIR WILLIAM DRAPER, KNIGHT OF THE BATH.

SIR,   *FEBRUARY* 21. 1769.

I SHOULD juftly be fufpeÆed of aÆing upon motives of more than
common enmity to Lord Granby, if I continued to give you frefh
materials or occafion for writing in his defence. Individuals who
hate, and the public who defpife, have read *your* letters, Sir William,
with infinitely more fatisfaÆion than mine. Unfortunately for him,
his reputation, like that unhappy country to which you refer me for
his laft military atchievements, has fuffered more by his friends than
his enemies. In mercy to him, let us drop the fubjeÆ. For my own
part, I willingly leave it to the public to determine whether your
vindication of your friend has been as able and judicious, as it was
certainly well intended; and you, I think, may be fatisfied with the
warm acknowledgements he already owes you for making him the
principal figure in a piece, in which, but for your amicable affiftance,
he might have paffed without particular notice or diftinÆion.

IN juftice to your friends, let your future labours be confined to

the care of your own reputation. Your declaration, that you are happy in feeing young noblemen *come among us*, is liable to two objections. With refpect to Lord Percy, it means nothing, for he was already in the army. He was aid-de-camp to the King, and had the
rank of colonel. A regiment therefore could not make him a more
military man, though it made him richer, and probably at the expence of fome brave, deferving, friendlefs officer. The other concerns yourfelf. After felling the companions of your victory in one
inftance, and after felling your profeffion in the other, by what authority do you prefume to call yourfelf a foldier? The plain evidence of facts is fuperior to all declarations. Before you were appointed to the 16th regiment, your complaints were a diftrefs to government; from that moment you were filent. The conclufion is
inevitable. You infinuate to us that your ill ftate of health obliged
you to quit the fervice. The retirement neceffary to repair a broken
conftitution would have been as good a reafon for not accepting, as
for refigning, the command of a regiment. There is certainly an error of the prefs, or an affected obfcurity in that paragraph, where
you fpeak of your bargain with Colonel Gifborne. Inftead of attempting to anfwer what I do not really underftand, permit me to
explain to the public what I really know. In exchange for your regiment, you accepted of a colonel's half-pay (at leaft L.220 a-year),
and an annuity of L.200 for your own and Lady Draper's life joint-
ly: And is this the lofing bargain, which you would reprefent to us,
as if you had given up an income of L.800 a-year for L.380? Was
it decent, was it honourable, in a man who pretends to love the army, and calls himfelf a foldier, to make a traffic of the royal favour,
and turn the higheft honour of an active profeffion into a fordid provifion for himfelf and his family? It were unworthy of me to prefs
you farther. The contempt with which the whole army heard of
the manner of your retreat, affures me, that, as your conduct was not
juftified by precedent, it will never be thought an example for imi-
tation.

G

THE laft and moft important queftion remains. When you receive
your half-pay, do you, or do you not, take a folemn oath, or fign a
declaration upon your honour, to the following effect? *That you do
not actually hold any place of profit, civil or military, under his Majefty.*
The charge which the queftion plainly conveys againft you is of fo
fhocking a complexion, that I fincerely wifh you may be able to anfwer it well, not merely for the colour of your reputation, but for
your own peace of mind.

JUNIUS.

LETTER VI.

TO JUNIUS.

SIR,   *FEBRUARY* 27. 1769.

I HAVE a very fhort anfwer for Junius's important queftion: I do
not either take an oath, or declare upon honour, that I have no *place*
of profit, *civil* or military, when I receive the half-pay as an Irifh colonel. My moft gracious Sovereign gives it me as a penfion; he was
pleafed to think I deferved it. The annuity of L.200 Irifh, and the
equivalent for the half-pay, together produce no more than L.380
per annum, clear of fees and perquifites of office. I receive L.167
from my government of Yarmouth—Total L.547 per annum. My
confcience is much at eafe in thefe particulars; my friends need not
blufh for me.

JUNIUS makes much and frequent ufe of interrogations: They
are arms that may be eafily turned againft himfelf. I could, by malicious interrogation, difturb the peace of the moft virtuous man in
the kingdom. I could take the decalogue, and fay to one man, Did
yo never fteal? to the next, Did you never commit murder? and to
Junius himfelf, who is putting my life and conduct to the rack, Did

you never bear falfe witnefs againft thy neighbour? Junius muft eafily fee, that, unlefs he affirms to the contrary in his real name, fome
people who may be as ignorant of him as I am, will be apt to fufpect him of having deviated a little from the truth : Therefore let
Junius afk no more queftions. You bite againft a file : Ceafe, viper.

W. D.

LETTER VII.

TO SIR WILLIAM DRAPER, KNIGHT OF THE BATH.

SIR, *MARCH* 3. 1769.

AN academical education has given you an unlimited command
over the moft beautiful figures of fpeech. Mafks, hatchets, racks,
and vipers, dance through your letters in all the mazes of metapho-
rical confufion. Thefe are the gloomy companions of a difturbed
imagination ; the melancholy madnefs of poetry, without the infpi-
ration. I will not contend with you in point of compofition. You
are a fcholar, Sir William ; and, if I am truly informed, you write
Latin with almoft as much purity as Englifh. Suffer me then, for I
am a plain unlettered man, to continue that ftile of interrogation
which fuits my capacity, and to which, confidering the readinefs of
your anfwers, you ought to have no objection. Even Mr. Bingley *
promifes to anfwer, if put to the torture.

Do you then really think, that, if I were to afk a *moft virtuous
man* whether he ever committed theft or murder, it would difturb
his peace of mind? Such a queftion might perhaps difcompofe the

---

* This man, being committed by the Court of King's Bench for a contempt, voluntarily made oath,
that he would never anfwer interrogatories, unlefs he fhould be put to the torture.

gravity of his mufcles, but I believe it would little affect the tran-
quillity of his confcience. Examine your own breaft, Sir William,
and you will difcover, that reproaches and inquiries have no power
to afflict either the man of unblemifhed integrity, or the abandoned
profligate. It is the middle compound character which alone is vul-
nerable ; the man who, without firmnefs enough to avoid a difhonourable action, has feeling enough to be afhamed of it.

I THANK you for the hint of the decalogue, and fhall take an opportunity of applying it to fome of your moft virtuous friends in
both houfes of parliament.

You feem to have dropped the affair of your regiment ; fo let it
reft. When you are appointed to another, I dare fay you will not fell
it either for a grofs fum, or for an annuity upon lives.

I AM truly glad (for really, Sir William, I am not your enemy,
nor did I begin this conteft with you) that you have been able to
clear yourfelf of a crime, though at the expence of the higheft indif-
cretion. You fay that your half-pay was given you by way of penfion. I will not dwell upon the fingularity of uniting in your own
perfon two forts of provifion, which, in their own nature, and in all
military and parliamentary views, are incompatible ; but I call upon
you to juftify that declaration, wherein you charge your Sovereign
with having done an act in your favour notorioufly againft law.—
The half-pay, both in Ireland and England, is appropriated by parliament ; and if it be given to perfons who, like you, are legally incapable of holding it, it is a breach of law. It would have been more
decent in you to have called this difhonourable tranfaction by its
true name, a job to accommodate two perfons, by particular intereft
and management at the caftle. What fenfe muft government have
had of your fervices, when the rewards they have given you are only a difgrace to you.

AND now, Sir William, I shall take my leave of you for ever. Motives very different from any apprehenfion of your refentment, make it impoffible you fhould ever know me. In truth, you have fome reafon to hold yourfelf indebted to me. From the leffons I have given you, you may.colle&t a profitable inftru&tion for your future life. They will either teach you fo to regulate your condu&t, as to be able to fet the moft malicious inquiries at defiance; or, if that be a loft hope, they will teach you prudence enough not to attra&t the public attention to a chara&ter, which will only pafs without cenfure, when it paffes without obfervation.

JUNIUS.

It has been faid, I believe truly, that it was fignified to Sir William Draper, as the requeft of Lord Granby, that he fhould defift from writing in his Lordfhip's defence. Sir William Draper certainly drew *Junius* forward to fay more of Lord Granby's chara&ter than he originally intended. He was reduced to the dilemma of either being totally filenced, or of fupporting his firft letter. Whether Sir William had a right to reduce him to this dilemma, or to call upon him for his name, after a voluntary attack on *his* fide, are queftions fubmitted to the candour of the public. The death of Lord Granby was lamented by *Junius.* He undoubtedly owed fome compenfations to the public, and feemed determined to acquit himfelf of them. In private life, he was unqueftionably that good man, who, for the intereft of his country, ought to have been a great one. *Bonum virum facile dixeris; magnum libenter.* I fpeak of him now without partiality :—I never fpoke of him with refentment. His miftakes, in public condu&t, did not arife either from want of fentiment, or want of judgment, but in general from the difficulty of faying NO to the bad people who furrounded him.

As for the reft, the friends of Lord Granby fhould remember, that he himfelf thought proper to condemn, retra&t, and difavow, by a moft folemn declaration in the Houfe of Commons, that very fyftem of political condu&t which *Junius* had held forth to the difapprobation of the public.

LETTER VIII.

TO HIS GRACE THE DUKE OF GRAFTON.

MY LORD,   *MARCH* 18. 1769.

BEFORE you were placed at the head of affairs, it had been a maxim of the Englifh government, not unwillingly admitted by the people, that every ungracious or fevere exertion of the prerogative fhould be placed to the account of the Minifter; but that, whenever.

an act of grace or benevolence was to be performed, the whole merit of it fhould be attributed to the Sovereign himfelf *. It was a wife
doctrine, my Lord, and equally advantageous to the King and his
fubjects; for, while it preferved that fufpicious attention with which
the people ought always to examine the conduct of minifters, it tended at the fame time rather to increafe than diminifh their attachment
to the perfon of their Sovereign. If there be not a fatality attending
every meafure you are concerned in, by what treachery, or by what
excefs of folly, has it happened, that thofe ungracious acts which
have diftinguifhed your adminiftration, and which I doubt not were
entirely your own, fhould carry with them a ftrong appearance of
perfonal intereft, and even of perfonal enmity, in a quarter where no
fuch intereft or enmity can be fuppofed to exift without the higheft
injuftice and the higheft difhonour? On the other hand, by what injudicious management have you contrived it, that the only act of
mercy to which you have ever advifed your Sovereign, far from ad-
ding to the luftre of a character truly gracious and benevolent, fhould
be received with univerfal difapprobation and difguft? I fhall confider it as a minifterial meafure, becaufe it is an odious one; and as
your meafure, my Lord Duke, becaufe you are the minifter.

As long as the trial of this chairman was depending, it was natural enough that government fhould give him every poffible encouragement and fupport. The honourable fervice for which he was
hired, and the fpirit with which he performed it, made a common
caufe between your Grace and him. The minifter, who, by fecret
corruption, invades the freedom of elections, and the ruffian, who,
by open violence, deftroys that freedom, are embarked in the fame
bottom. They have the fame interefts, and mutually feel for each
other. To do juftice to your Grace's humanity, you felt for M'Quirk

---

* Les rois ne fe font refervé que les graces. Ils renvoient les condamnations vers leurs officiers.
MONTESQUIEU.

as you ought to do ; and if you had been contented to affift him in-
directly, without a notorious denial of juftice, or openly infulting the
fenfe of the nation, you might have fatisfied every duty of political
friendfhip, without commuting the honour of your Sovereign, or hazarding the reputation of his government.   But when this unhappy
man had been folemnly tried, convicted, and condemned ; when it
appeared that he had been frequently employed in the fame fervices,
and that no excufe for him could be drawn either from the innocence of his former life or the fimplicity of his character ; was it not
hazarding too much to interpofe the ftrength of the prerogative between this felon and the juftice of his country * ?   You ought to have

---

* *Whitehall, March* 11. 1769.—His Majefty has been gracioufly pleafed to extend his royal mercy to
Edward M'Quirk, found guilty of the murder of George Clarke, as appears by his royal warrant to the
tenor following :.

GEORGE R.

WHEREAS a doubt had arifen in our royal breaft concerning the evidence of the death of George Clarke,
from the reprefentations of William Bromfield, Efq. furgeon, and Solomou Starling, apothecary ; both of
whom, as has been reprefented to us, attended the deceafed before his death, and expreffed their opinions
that he did not die of the blow he received at Brentford : And whereas it appears to us, that neither of
the faid perfons were produced as witneffes upon the trial, though the faid Solomon Starling had been
examined before the coroner ; and the only perfon called to prove that the death of the faid George
Clarke was occafioned by the faid blow, was John Foot, furgeon, who never faw the deceafed till after
his death : We thought fit thereupon to refer the faid reprefentations, together with the report of the Recorder of our city of London, of the evidence given by Richard and William Beale, and the faid John
Foot, on the trial of Edward Quirk, otherwife called Edward Kirk, otherwife called Edward M'Quirk, .
for the murder of the faid Clarke, to the mafter, wardens, and the reft of the court of examiners of the
furgeons company, commanding them likewife to take fuch further examination of the faid perfons fo
reprefenting, and of faid John Foot, as they might think neceffary, together with the premifes above
mentioned, to form and report to us their opinion, " Whether it did or did not appear to them, that the
faid George Clarke died in confequence of the blow he received in the riot at Brentford on the 8th of
December laft."   And the faid court of examiners of the furgeons company having thereupon reported
to us their opinion, " That it did not appear to them that he did ;" we have thought proper to extend
our royal mercy to him the faid Edward Quirk, otherwife Edward Kirk, otherwife called Edward M'Quirk,
and to grant him our free pardon for the murder of the faid George Clarke, of which he has been found
guilty.   Our will and pleafure therefore is, That he the faid Edward Quirk, otherwife called Kirk, otherwife called Edward M'Quirk, be inferted, for the faid murder, in our firft and next general pardon that
fhall come out for the poor convicts of Newgate, without any condition whatfoever ; and that in the mean
time you take bail for his appearance, in order to plead our faid pardon.   And for fo doing this fhall be
your warrant.

Given at our court at St James's the 10th day of March 1769, in the ninth year of our reign.
                    By his Majefty's command,
                                                    ROCHFORD.

To our trufty and well-beloved James Eyre, Efq. Recorder of our city
   of London, the Sheriffs of our faid city and county of Middlefex,
   and all others whom it may concern.

known that an example of this fort was never fo neceffary as at prefent; and certainly you muft have known that the lot could not
have fallen upon a more guilty objeᶜt. What fyftem of government
is this? You are perpetually complaining of the riotous difpofition of
the lower clafs of people; yet, when the laws have given you the
means of making an example, in every fenfe unexceptionable, and
by far the moft likely to awe the multitude, you pardon the offence,
and are not afhamed to give the fanᶜtion of government to the riots
you complain of, and even to future murders. You are partial perhaps to the military mode of execution; and had rather fee a fcore
of thefe wretches butchered by the guards, than one of them fuffer
death by regular courfe of law. How does it happen, my Lord, that,
in *your* hands, even the mercy of the prerogative is cruelty and op-
preffion to the fubjeᶜt?

THE meafure, it feems, was fo extraordinary, that you thought it
neceffary to give fome reafons for it to the public. Let them be fairly examined.

1. YOU fay, that *Meff. Bromfield and Starling were not examined
at M'Quirk's trial.* I will tell your Grace why they were not. They
muft have been examined upon oath; and it was forefeen, that their
evidence would either not benefit or might be prejudicial to the pri-
foner: Otherwife, is it conceiveable that his counfel fhould negleᶜt
to call in fuch material evidence?

YOU fay, that *Mr Foot did not fee the deceafed until after his death.*
A furgeon, my Lord, muft know very little of his profeffion, if, upon examining a wound or a contufion, he cannot determine whether it was mortal or not. While the party is alive, a furgeon will
be cautious of pronouncing; whereas, by the death of the patient,
he is enabled to confider both caufe and effeᶜt in one view, and to
fpeak with a certainty confirmed by experience.

YET we are to thank your Grace for the eftablifhment of a new tribunal. Your *inquifitio poft mortem* is unknown to the laws of England, and does honour to your invention. The only material objection to it is, that, if Mr. Foot's evidence was infufficient, becaufe he did not examine the wound till after the death of the party, much lefs can a negative opinion, given by gentlemen who never faw the body of Mr Clarke, either before or after his deceafe, authorife you to fuperfede the verdict of a jury, and the fentence of the law.

Now, my Lord, let me afk you, Has it never occurred to your Grace, while you were withdrawing this defperate wretch from that juftice which the laws had awarded, and which the whole people of England demanded againft him, that there is another man, who is the favourite of his country, whofe pardon would have been accepted with gratitude, whofe pardon would have healed all our divifions ? Have you quite forgotten that this man was once your Grace's friend ? or is it to murderers only that you will extend the mercy of the Crown ?

THESE are queftions you will not anfwer, nor is it neceffary.— The character of your private life, and the tenor of your public conduct, is an anfwer to them all.

JUNIUS.

LETTER IX.

TO HIS GRACE THE DUKE OF GRAFTON.

MY LORD,   *APRIL* 10. 1769.

I HAVE fo good an opinion of your Grace's difcernment, that, when the author of the vindication of your conduct affures us, that

H

he writes from his own mere motion, without the leaft authority
from your Grace, I fhould be ready enough to believe him, but for
one fatal mark which feems to be fixed upon every meafure in which
either your perfonal or your political charaƈter is concerned. Your
firft attempt to fupport Sir William Proƈtor ended in the eleƈtion of
Mr. Wilkes; the fecond infured fuccefs to Mr. Glynn. The extraordinary ftep you took to make Sir James Lowther lord paramount of
Cumberland has ruined his intereft in that county for ever. The
houfe lift of direƈtors was curfed with the concurrence of government; and even the miferable Dingley * could not efcape the mif-
fortune of your Grace's proteƈtion. With this uniform experience
before us, we are authorifed to fufpeƈt, that, when a pretended vindication of your principles and conduƈt in reality contains the bit-
tereft refleƈtions upon both, it could not have been written without
your immediate direƈtion and affiftance. The author indeed calls God
to witnefs for him, with all the fincerity, and in the very terms of
an Irifh evidence, *to the beft of his knowledge and belief.* My Lord,
you fhould not encourage thefe appeals to heaven. The pious Prince
from whom you are fuppofed to defcend made fuch frequent ufe of
them in his public declarations, that, at laft, the people alfo found it
neceffary to appeal to heaven in their turn. Your adminiftration has
driven us into circumftances of equal diftrefs; beware at leaft how
you remind us of the remedy.

YOU have already much to anfwer for: You have provoked this
unhappy gentleman to play the fool once more in public life, in fpite
of his years and infirmities; and to fhow us, that, as you yourfelf are
a fingular inftance of youth without fpirit, the man who defends you
is a no lefs remarkable example of age without the benefit of expe-

---

* This unfortunate perfon had been perfuaded by the Duke of Graftop to fet up for Middlefex, his
Grace being determined to feat him in the Houfe of Commons, if he had but a fingle vote. It happened
unluckily that he could not prevail upon any one freeholder to put him in nomination.

rience. To follow fuch a writer minutely, would, like his own periods, be a labour without end. The fubject too has been already dif-
cuffed, and is fufficiently underftood. I cannot help obferving, however, that, when the pardon of M'Quirk was the principal charge
againft you, it would have been but a decent compliment to your
Grace's underftanding, to have defended you upon your own principles. What credit does a man deferve, who tells us plainly, that
the facts fet forth in the King's proclamation were not the true motives on which the pardon was granted; and that he wifhes that
thofe chirurgical reports, which firft gave occafion to certain doubts
in the royal breaft, had not been laid before his Majefty. You fee,
my Lord, that even your friends cannot defend your actions, without changing your principles, nor juftify a deliberate meafure of government, without contradicting the main affertion on which it was
founded.

THE conviction of M'Quirk had reduced you to a dilemma, in
which it was hardly poffible for you to reconcile your political intereft with your duty. You were obliged either to abandon an active
ufeful partizan, or to protect a felon from public juftice. With your
ufual fpirit, you preferred your intereft to every other confideration ;
and, with your ufual judgment, you founded your determination
upon the only motives which fhould not have been given to the public.

I HAVE frequently cenfured Mr. Wilkes's conduct, yet your advocate reproaches me with having devoted myfelf to the fervice of fe-
dition. Your Grace can beft inform us, for which of Mr. Wilkes's
good qualities you firft honoured him with your friendfhip, or how
long it was before you difcovered thofe bad ones in him, at which,
it feems, your delicacy was offended. Remember, my Lord, that you
continued your connection with Mr. Wilkes long after he had been
convicted of thofe crimes which you have fince taken pains to repre-

fent in the blackeft colours of blafphemy and treafon. How unlucky
is it that the firft inftance you have given us of a fcrupulous regard
to decorum is united with the breach of a moral obligation ! For my
own part, my Lord, I am proud to affirm, that, if I had been weak
enough to form fuch a friendfhip, I would never have been bafe
enough to betray it. But, let Mr. Wilkes's character be what it may,
this at leaft is certain, that, circumftanced as he is with regard to the
public, even his vices plead for him. The people of England have
too much difcernment to fuffer your Grace to take advantage of the
failings of a private character to eftablifh a precedent by which the
public liberty is affected, and which you may hereafter, with equal
eafe and fatisfaction, employ to the ruin of the beft men in the kingdom.—Content yourfelf, my Lord, with the many advantages which
the unfullied purity of your own character has given you over your
unhappy deferted friend. Avail yourfelf of all the unforgiving piety
of the court you live in, and blefs God that you " are not as other
men are, extortioners, unjuft, adulterers, or even as this publican."
In a heart void of feeling, the laws of honour and good faith may be
violated with impunity, and there you may fafely indulge your genius. But the laws of England fhall not be violated, even by your
holy zeal to opprefs a finner; and though you have fucceeded in
making him a tool, you fhall not make him the victim of your ambition.   JUNIUS.

LETTER X.

TO MR. EDWARD WESTON.

SIR,   *APRIL* 21. 1769.

I SAID you were an old man without the benefit of experience. It
feems you are alfo a volunteer with the ftipend of twenty commif-

fions; and, at a period when all profpects are at an end, you are ftill looking forward to rewards which you cannot enjoy. No man is better acquainted with the bounty of government than you are.

———ton impudence,
, Temeraire vieillard, aura fa recompenfe.

BUT I will not defcend to an altercation either with the impotence of your age or the peevifhnefs of your difeafes. Your pamphlet, ingenious as it is, has been fo little read, that the public cannot know how far you have a right to give me the lie, without the following citation of your own words.

Page 6—" 1. THAT he is perfuaded that the motives which he (Mr. Wefton) has alleged, muft appear fully fufficient, with or without the opinions of the furgeons.

" 2. THAT thofe very motives MUST HAVE BEEN the foundation on which the Earl of Rochford thought proper, &c.

" 3. THAT he CANNOT BUT REGRET that the Earl of Rochford feems to have thought proper to lay the chirurgical reports before the King, in preference to all the other fufficient motives," &c.

LET the public determine whether this be defending government on their principles or your own.

THE ftile and language you have adopted are, I confefs, not ill fuited to the elegance of your own manners, or to the dignity of the caufe you have undertaken. Every common dauber writes rafcal and villain under his pictures, becaufe the pictures themfelves have neither character nor refemblance. But the works of a mafter require no index: His features and colouring are taken from nature: The impreffion they make is immediate and uniform; nor is it poffible to miftake his characters, whether they reprefent the treachery of a minifter, or the abufed fimplicity of a king.

JUNIUS.

LETTER XI.

TO HIS GRACE THE DUKE OF GRAFTON.

MY LORD,   *APRIL* 24. 1769.

THE fyftem you feemed to have adopted when Lord Chatham un-expectedly left you at the head of affairs gave us no promife of that uncommon exertion of vigour, which has fince illuftrated your cha-racter and diftinguifhed your adminiftration. Far from difcovering a fpirit bold enough to invade the firft rights of the people and the firft principles of the conftitution, you were fcrupulous of exercifing even thofe powers with which the executive branch of the legiflature is legally invefted. We have not yet forgotten how long Mr. Wilkes was fuffered to appear at large, nor how long he was at liberty to canvafs for the city and county, with all the terrors of an outlawry hanging over him. Our gracious Sovereign has not yet forgotten the extraordinary care you took of his dignity, and of the fafety of his perfon, when, at a crifis which courtiers affected to call alarming, you left the metropolis expofed, for two nights together, to every fpecies of riot and diforder. The fecurity of the royal refidence from infult was then fufficiently provided for in Mr. Conway's firmnefs, and Lord Weymouth's difcretion ; while the prime minifter of Great Britain, in a rural retirement, and in the arms of faded beauty, had loft all memory of his Sovereign, his country, and himfelf. In thefe inftances you might have acted with vigour, for you would have had the fanction of the laws to fupport you. The friends of government might have defended you without fhame ; and moderate men, who wiſh well to the peace and good order of ſociety, might have had a pretence for applauding your conduct. But theſe, it ſeems, were not occaſions worthy of your Grace's interpoſition. You reſerved the proofs of your intrepid ſpirit for trials of greater hazard and importance ; and now, as if the moſt diſgraceful relaxation of the executive authority had given you a claim of credit to indulge in exceſſes ſtill more dangerous, you ſeem determined to compenſate amply for your former negligence, and to balance the non-execution of the laws with a breach of the conſtitution. From one extreme you ſuddenly ſtart to the other, without leaving, between the weakneſs and the fury of the paſſions, one moment's interval for the firmneſs of the underſtanding.

THESE obſervations, general as they are, might eaſily be extended into a faithful hiſtory of your Grace's adminiſtration, and perhaps may be the employment of a future hour. But the buſineſs of the preſent moment will not ſuffer me to look back to a ſeries of events, which ceaſe to be intereſting or important, becauſe they are ſucceeded by a meaſure ſo ſingularly daring, that it excites all our attention, and engroſſes all our reſentment.

YOUR patronage of Mr. Luttrell has been crowned with ſuccefs. With this precedent before you, with the principles on which it was eſtabliſhed, and with a future Houſe of Commons, perhaps leſs virtuous than the preſent, every county in England, under the auſpices of the treaſury, may be repreſented as completely as the county of Middleſex. Poſterity will be indebted to your Grace for not contenting yourſelf with a temporary expedient, but entailing upon them the immediate bleſſings of your adminiſtration. Boroughs were already too much at the mercy of government. Counties could neither be purchaſed nor intimidated. But their ſolemn determined election may be rejected, and the man they deteſt may be appointed, by another choice, to repreſent them in parliament. Yet it is admitted,, that the Sheriffs obeyed the laws and performed their duty *. The return they made muft have been legal and valid, or undoubtedly they would have been cenfured for making it. With every good na-tured allowance for your Grace's youth and inexperience, there are fome things which you cannot but know : You cannot but know, that the right of the freeholders to adhere to their choice (even fup-pofing it improperly exerted) was as clear and indifputable as that of the Houfe of Commons to exclude one of their own members : Nor is it poffible for you not to fee the wide diftance there is be-tween the negative power of rejecting one man, and the pofitive power of appointing another. The right of expulfion, in the moft favourable fenfe, is no more than the cuftom of parliament. The right of election is the very effence of the conftitution. To violate that right, and much more to transfer it to any other fet of men, is a ftep leading immediately to the diffolution of all government. So far forth as it operates, it conftitutes a Houfe of Commons which *does not* reprefent the people. A Houfe of Commons fo formed would involve a contradiction and the groffeft confufion of ideas ; but there are fome minifters, my Lord, whofe views can only be anfwered by reconciling abfurdities, and making the fame propofition, which is falfe and abfurd in argument, true in fact.

THIS meafure, my Lord, is however attended with one confequence favourable to the people, which, I am perfuaded, you did not fore-fee §. While the conteft lay between the miniftry and Mr. Wilkes, his fituation and private character gave you advantages over him, which common candour, if not the memory of your former friend-fhip, fhould have forbidden you to make ufe of. To religious men, you had an opportunity of exaggerating the irregularities of his paft life ; to moderate men, you held forth the pernicious confequences

---

* Sir Fletcher Norton, when it was propofed to punifh the Sheriffs, declared in the Houfe of Commons, that they, in returning Mr Wilkes, had done no more than their duty.

§ The reader is defired to mark this prophecy. .

of faction. Men, who, with this character, looked no farther than to
the object before them, were not diffatisfied at feeing Mr. Wilkes excluded from parliament. You have now taken care to fhift the queftion, or, rather, you have created a new one, in which Mr. Wilkes
is no more concerned than any other Englifh gentleman. You have
united this country againft you on one grand conftitutional point,
on the decifion of which our exiftence, as a free people, abfolutely
depends. You have afferted, not in words but in fact, that the reprefentation in parliament does not depend upon the choice of the freeholders. If fuch a cafe can poffibly happen once, it may happen frequently; it may happen always;—and if three hundred votes, by
any mode of reafoning whatfoever, can prevail againft twelve hundred, the fame reafoning would equally have given Mr. Luttrell his
feat with ten votes, or even with one. The confequences of this attack upon the conftitution are too plain and palpable not to alarm
the dulleft apprehenfion. I truft you will find that the people of England are neither deficient in fpirit nor underftanding, though you
have treated them as if they had neither fenfe to feel, nor fpirit to
refent. We have reafon to thank God and our anceftors, that there
never yet was a minifter in this country who could ftand the iffue of
fuch a conflict; and, with every prejudice in favour of your inten-
tions, I fee no fuch abilities in your Grace as fhould entitle you to
fucceed in an enterprize, in which the ableft and bafeft of your predeceffors have found their deftruction. You may continue to deceive
your gracious mafter with falfe reprefentations of the temper and
condition of his fubjects: You may command a venal vote, becaufe
it is the common eftablifhed appendage of your office. But never
hope that the freeholders will make a tame furrender of their rights,
or that an Englifh army will join with you in overturning the li-
berties of their country. They know that their firft duty, as citizens,
is paramount to all fubfequent engagements; nor will they prefer
the difcipline or even the honours of their profeffion to thofe facred

I

original rights, which belonged to them before they were foldiers, and which they claim and poffefs as the birth-right of Englifhmen..

RETURN, my Lord, before it be too late, to that eafy infipid fyf- tem which you firft fet out with. Take back your miftrefs *;—the name of friend may be fatal to her, for it leads to treachery and per- fecution. Indulge the people. Attend Newmarket. Mr. Luttrell may again vacate his feat; and Mr. Wilkes, if not perfecuted, will foon be forgotten. To be weak and inactive is fafer than to be daring and criminal; and wide is the diftance between a riot of the populace and a convulfion of the whole kingdom. You may live to make the experiment, but no honeft man can wifh you fhould furvive it.

JUNIUS..

LETTER XII..

TO HIS GRACE THE DUKE OF GRAFTON..

MY LORD,   *MAY* 30. 1769.

IF the meafures in which you have been moft fuccefsful had been fupported by any tolerable appearance of argument, I fhould have thought my time not ill employed in continuing to examine your conduct as a minifter, and ftating it fairly to the public. But when I fee queftions of the higheft national importance carried as they have been, and the firft principles of the conftitution openly violated, with- out argument or decency, I confefs I give up the caufe in defpair.— The meaneft of your predeceffors had abilities fufficient to give a co- lour to their meafures. If they invaded the rights of the people, they

---

* The Duke, about this time, had feparated himfelf from Ann Parfons; but propofed to continue united with her, on fome platonic terms of friendfhip, which fhe rejected with contempt. His bafenefs to this woman is beyond defcription or belief.

did not dare to offer a direct infult to their underftanding; and, in former times, the moft venal parliaments made it a condition, in their bargain with the minifter, that he fhould furnifh them with fome plaufible pretences for felling their country and themfelves.—— You have had the merit of introducing a more compendious fyftem of government and logic. You neither addrefs yourfelf to the paffions, nor to the underftanding, but fimply to the touch. You apply yourfelf immediately to the feelings of your friends, who, contrary to the forms of parliament, never enter heartily into a debate, until they have divided.

RELINQUISHING, therefore, all idle views of amendment to your Grace, or of benefit to the public, let me be permitted to confider your character and conduct merely as a fubject of curious fpeculation. There is fomething in both which diftinguifhes you not only from all other minifters, but all other men; it is not that you do wrong by defign, but that you fhould never do right by miftake. It is not that your indolence and your activity have been equally mifapplied; but that the firft uniform principle, or if I may call it the genius of your life, fhould have carried you through every poffible change and contradiction of conduct, without the momentary imputation or colour of a virtue; and that the wildeft fpirit of inconfiftency fhould never once have betrayed you into a wife or honourable action. This, I own, gives an air of fingularity to your fortune, as well as to your difpofition. Let us look back together to a fcene in which a mind like yours will find nothing to repent of. Let us try, my Lord, how well you have fupported the various relations in which you ftood, to your fovereign, your country, your friends, and yourfelf. Give us, if it be poffible, fome excufe to pofterity, and to ourfelves, for fubmitting to your adminiftration. If not the abilities of a great minifter, if not the integrity of a patriot, or the fidelity of a friend, fhow us at leaft the firmnefs of a man. For the fake of your miftrefs, the lover fhall be fpared. I will not lead her into public, as

you have done, nor will I infult the memory of departed beauty.—
Her fex, which alone made her amiable in your eyes, makes her refpectable in mine.

THE character of the reputed anceftors of fome men, has made it
poffible for their defcendents to be vicious in the extreme, without
being degenerate. Thofe of your Grace, for inftance, left no diftref-
fing examples of virtue, even to their legitimate pofterity; and you
may look back with pleafure to an illuftrious pedigree, in which he-
raldry has not left a fingle good quality upon record to infult or up-
braid you. You have better proofs of your defcent, my Lord, than
the regifter of a marriage, or any troublefome inheritance of reputation. There are fome hereditary ftrokes of character, by which a family may be as clearly diftinguifhed as by the blackeft features of the
human face. Charles the Firft lived and died a hypocrite. Charles
the Second was a hypocrite of another fort, and fhould have died upon the fame fcaffold. At the diftance of a century, we fee their different characters happily revived and blended in your Grace. Sullen
and fevere without religion, profligate without gaiety, you live like
Charles the Second, without being an amiable companion; and, for
aught I know, may die as his father did, without the reputation of a
martyr.

YOU had already taken your degrees with credit in thofe fchools in
which the Englifh nobility are formed to virtue, when you were introduced to Lord Chatham's protection *. From Newmarket, White's,
and the oppofition, he gave you to the world with an air of popularity, which young men ufually fet out with, and feldom preferve:
Grave and plaufible enough to be thought fit for bufinefs; too young
for treachery; and, in fhort, a patriot of no unpromifing expecta-

* To underftand thefe paffages, the reader is referred to a noted pamphlet, called, The Hiftory of the
Minority.

tions. Lord Chatham was the earlieft obje{$\mathrm{\&}$}t of your political wonder and attachment; yet you deferted him, upon the firft hopes that offered of an equal fhare of power with Lord Rockingham. When the Duke of Cumberland's firft negotiation failed, and when the favourite was pufhed to the laft extremity, you faved him, by joining with an adminiftration in which Lord Chatham had refufed to engage.— Still, however, he was your friend;—and you are yet to explain to the world, why you confented to aft without him; or why, after uniting with Lord Rockingham, you deferted and betrayed him.— You complained that no meafures were taken to fatisfy your patron; and that your friend Mr. Wilkes, who had fuffered fo much for the party, had been abandoned to his fate. They have fince contributed not a little to your prefent plenitude of power; yet, I think, Lord Chatham has lefs reafon than ever to be fatisfied; and as for Mr. Wilkes, it is perhaps the greateft misfortune of his life, that you fhould have fo many compenfations to make in the clofet for your former friendfhip with him. Your gracious mafter underftands your charaðter; and makes you a perfecutor, becaufe you have been a friend.

LORD CHATHAM formed his laft adminiftration upon principles which you certainly concurred in, or you could never have been placed at the head of the treafury. By deferting thofe principles, and by aðting in direð contradiðtion to them, in which he found you were fecretly fupported in the clofet, you foon forced him to leave you to yourfelf, and to withdraw his name from an adminiftration which had been formed on the credit of it. You had then a profpeð of friendfhips better fuited to your genius, and more likely to fix your difpofition. Marriage is the point on which every rake is ftationary at laft; and truly, my Lord, you may well be weary of the circuit you have taken; for you have now fairly travelled through every fign in the political zodiac, from the Scorpion, in which you ftung

Lord Chatham, to the hopes of a Virgin * in the houfe of Bloomf-
bury. One would think that you had had fufficient experience of the
frailty of nuptial engagements, or, at leaft, that fuch a friendfhip as
the Duke of Bedford's might have been fecured to you by the aufpicious marriage of your late Duchefs with his nephew §. But ties of
this tender nature cannot be drawn too clofe ; and it may poffibly be
a part of the Duke of Bedford's ambition, after making *her* an honeft woman, to work a miracle of the fame fort upon your Grace.
This worthy nobleman has long dealt in virtue. There has been a
large confumption of it in his own family ; and, in the way of traffic, I dare fay, he has bought and fold more than half the reprefentative integrity of the nation.

IN a political view, this union is not imprudent. The favour of
princes is a perifhable commodity. You have now a ftrength fufficient to command the clofet ; and if it be neceffary to betray one
friendfhip more, you may fet even Lord Bute at defiance. Mr Stew-
art Mackenzie may poffibly remember what ufe the Duke of Bedford
ufually makes of his power ; and our gracious Sovereign, I doubt not,
rejoices at this firft appearance of union among his fervants. His
late Majefty, under the happy influence of a family connexion between his minifters, was relieved from the cares of the government.
A more active prince may perhaps obferve, with fufpicion, by what
degrees an artful fervant grows upon his mafter, from the firft unlimited profeffions of duty and attachment, to the painful reprefentation of the neceffity of the royal fervice, and foon, in regular pro-
greffion, to the humble infolence of dictating in all the obfequious
forms of peremptory fubmiffion. The interval is carefully employed
in forming connexions, creating interefts, collecting a party, and lay-
ing the foundation of double marriages ; until the deluded prince,

---

* His Grace had lately married Mifs Wrottefley, niece of the *Good Gertrude, Duchefs of Bedford.*

§ Mifs Liddell, after her divorce from the Duke, married Lord Upper Offory.

who thought he had found a creature proftituted to his fervice, and infignificant enough to be always dependent upon his pleafure, finds him at laft too ftrong to be commanded, and too formidable to be removed.

YOUR Grace's public conduct, as a minifter, is but the counter part of your private hiftory; the fame inconfiftency, the fame contradictions. In America we trace you, from the firft oppofition to the ftamp act, on principles of convenience, to Mr. Pitt's furrender of the right; then forward to Lord Rockingham's furrender of the fact; then back again to Lord Rockingham's declaration of the right; then forward to taxation with Mr. Townfhend; and in the laft inftance, from the gentle Conway's undetermined difcretion, to blood and compulfion with the Duke of Bedford: Yet, if we may believe the fimplicity of Lord North's eloquence, at the opening of next feffions you are once more to be the patron of America. Is this the wifdom of a great minifter? or is it the ominous vibration of a pendulum? Had you no opinion of your own, my Lord? or was it the gratification of betraying every party with which you have been united, and of deferting every political principle in which you had concurred?

YOUR enemies may turn their eyes without regret from this admirable fyftem of provincial government. They will find gratification enough in the furvey of your domeftic and foreign policy.

IF, inftead of difowning Lord Shelburne, the Britifh Court had interpofed with dignity and firmnefs, you know, my Lord, that Corfica would never have been invaded. The French faw the weaknefs of a diftracted miniftry, and were juftified in treating you with contempt. They would probably have yielded in the firft inftance, rather than hazard a rupture with this country; but, being once engaged, they cannot retreat without difhonour. Common fenfe fore-

fees confequences which have efcaped your Grace's penetration. Either we fuffer the French to make an acquifition, the importance of
which you have probably no conception of; or we oppofe them by
an underhand management, which only difgraces us in the eyes of
Europe, without anfwering any purpofe of policy or prudence.—
From fecret, indirect affiftance, a tranfition to fome more open decifive meafures becomes unavoidable; till at laft we find ourfelves principal in the war, and are obliged to hazard every thing for an object
which might have originally been obtained without expence or danger. I am not verfed in the politics of the north; but this I believe
is certain, that half the money you have diftributed to carry the expulfion of Mr. Wilkes, or even your fecretary's fhare in the laft fubfcrip-
tion, would have kept the Turks at your devotion. Was it economy,
my Lord? or did the coy refiftance you have conftantly met with in
the Britifh fenate make you defpair of corrupting the Divan? Your
friends indeed have the firft claim upon your bounty; but if five
hundred pounds a-year can be fpared in penfion to Sir John Moore,
it would not have difgraced you to have allowed fomething to the
fecret fervice of the public.

You will fay, perhaps, that the fituation of affairs at home demanded and engroffed the whole of your attention. Here, I confefs,
you have been active. An amiable accomplifhed prince afcends the
throne under the happieft of all aufpices, the acclamations and united
affections of his fubjects. The firft meafures of his reign, and even
the odium of a favourite, were not able to fhake their attachment.
Your fervices, my Lord, have been more fuccefsful. Since you were
permitted to take the lead, we have feen the natural effects of a fyftem of government at once both odious and contemptible. We have
feen the laws fometimes fcandaloufly relaxed, fometimes violently
ftretched beyond their tone. We have feen the perfon of the Sovereign infulted; and in profound peace, and with an undifputed title,
the fidelity of his fubjects brought by his own fervants into public

queftion *. Without abilities, refolution, or intereft, you have done more than Lord Bute could accomplifh with all Scotland at his heels.

.Your Grace, little anxious perhaps either for prefent or future reputation, will not defire to be handed down in thefe colours to po-fterity. You have reafon to flatter yourfelf that the memory of your adminiftration will furvive even the forms of a conftitution which our anceftors vainly hoped would be immortal; and as for your per-fonal character, I will not, for the honour of human nature, fuppofe that you can wifh to have it remembered. The condition of the pre-fent times is defperate indeed; but there is a debt due to thofe who come after us; and it is the hiftorian's office to punifh, though he cannot correct. I do not give you to pofterity as a pattern to imi-tate, but as an example to deter; and as your conduct comprehends every thing that a wife or honeft minifter fhould avoid, I mean to make you a negative inftruction to your fucceffors for ever.

JUNIUS.

LETTER XIII.

ADDRESSED TO THE PRINTER OF THE PUBLIC ADVERTISER.

SIR,   *JUNE* 12. 1769.

THE Duke of Grafton's friends, not finding it convenient to en-ter into a conteft with *Junius*, are now reduced to the laft melan-choly refource of defeated argument, the flat general charge of fcur-rility and falfehood. As for his ftyle, I fhall leave it to the critics.—

---

* The wife Duke, about this time, exerted all the influence of government to procure addreffes to fa-tisfy the King of the fidelity of his fubjects. They came in very thick from *Scotland*; but, after the appear-ance of this letter, we heard no more of them.

K

The truth of his facts is of more importance to the public. They are of such a nature, that I think a bare contradiction will have no weight with any man who judges for himself. Let us take them in the order in which they appear in his laſt letter.

1. HAVE not the firſt rights of the people, and the firſt principles of the conſtitution, been openly invaded, and the very name of an election made ridiculous, by the arbitrary appointment of Mr. Luttrell?

2. DID not the Duke of Grafton frequently lead his miſtreſs into public, and even place her at the head of his table, as if he had pulled down an ancient temple of Venus, and could bury all decency and ſhame under the ruins?—Is this the man who dares to talk of Mr. Wilkes's morals?

3. Is not the character of his preſumptive anceſtors as ſtrongly marked in him, as if he had deſcended from them in a direct legitimate line? The idea of his death is only prophetic; and what is prophecy but a narrative preceding the fact!

4. WAS not Lord Chatham the firſt who raiſed him to the rank and poſt of a miniſter, and the firſt whom he abandoned?

5. DID he not join with Lord Rockingham, and betray him?

6. WAS he not the boſom friend of Mr. Wilkes, whom he now purſues to deſtruction?

7. DID he not take his degrees with credit at Newmarket, White's, and the oppoſition?

8. AFTER deſerting Lord Chatham's principles, and ſacrificing his

friendſhip, is he not now cloſely united with a ſet of men, who, though they have occaſionally joined with all parties, have in every different ſituation, and at all times, been equally and conſtantly deteſted by this country?

9. HAS not Sir John Moore a penſion of five hundred pounds a-year?—This may probably be an acquittance of favours upon the turf; but is it poſſible for a miniſter to offer a groſſer outrage to a nation, which has ſo very lately cleared away the beggary of the civil liſt at the expence of more than half a million?

10. Is there any one mode of thinking or acting with reſpect to America, which the Duke of Grafton has not ſucceſſively adopted and abandoned?

11. Is there not a ſingular mark of ſhame ſet upon this man, who has ſo little delicacy and feeling as to ſubmit to the opprobrium of marrying a near relation of one who had debauched his wife?—In the name of decency, how are theſe amiable couſins to meet at their uncle's table? It will be a ſcene in Oedipus, without the diſtreſs. Is it wealth, or wit, or beauty—or is the amorous youth in love?

THE reſt is notorious: That Corſica has been ſacrificed to the French: That in ſome inſtances the laws have been ſcandalouſly relaxed, and in others daringly violated; and that the King's ſubjects have been called upon to aſſure him of their fidelity, in ſpite of the meaſures of his ſervants.

A WRITER, who builds his arguments upon facts ſuch as theſe, is not eaſily to be confuted. He is not to be anſwered by general aſſertions or general reproaches. He may want eloquence to amuſe and perſuade; but, ſpeaking truth, he muſt always convince.

K 2 'PHILO JUNIUS.

LETTER XIV.

ADDRESSED TO THE PRINTER OF THE PUBLIC ADVERTISER.

SIR,   *JUNE* 22. 1769.

THE name of *Old Noll* is deftined to be the ruin of the houfe of Stuart. There is an ominous fatality in it, which even the fpurious defcendents of the family cannot efcape. Oliver Cromwell had the merit of conducing Charles the Firft to the block. Your correfpondent OLD NOLL appears to have the fame defign upon the Duke of Grafton. His arguments confift better with the title he has affumed than with the principles he profeffes ; for, though he pretends to be an advocate for the Duke, he takes care to give us the beft reafons why his patron fhould regularly follow the fate of his prefumptive anceftor. Through the whole courfe of the Duke of Grafton's life I fee a ftrange endeavour to unite contradictions which cannot be reconciled. He marries to be divorced ; he keeps a miftrefs to remind him of conjugal endearments ; and he chufes fuch friends as it is virtue in him to defert. If it were poffible for the genius of that accomplifhed prefident, who pronounced fentence upon Charles the Firft, to be revived in fome modern fycophant *, his Grace, I doubt not, would by fympathy difcover him among the dregs of mankind, and take him for a guide in thofe paths which naturally conduct a minifter to the fcaffold.

THE affertion, that two thirds of the nation approve of the *acceptance* of Mr. Luttrell (for even *Old Noll* is too modeft to call it an election), can neither be maintained nor confuted by argument. It is a point of fact, on which every Englifh gentleman will determine

---

* It is hardly neceffary to remind the reader of the name of *Bradfhaw*.

for himfelf. As to lawyers, their profeffion is fupported by the in-
difcriminate defence of right and wrong; and I confefs I have not
that opinion of their knowledge or integrity, to think it neceffary
that they fhould decide for me upon a plain conftitutional queftion.
With refpect to the appointment of Mr. Luttrell, the chancellor has
never yet given any authentic opinion. Sir Fletcher Norton is indeed
an honeft, a very honeft man; and the attorney general is *ex officio*
the guardian of liberty, to take care, I prefume, that it fhall never
break out into a criminal excefs. Dr. Blackftone is folicitor to the
Queen. The Doctor recollected that he had a place to preferve,
though he forgot that he had a reputation to lofe. We have now
the good fortune to underftand the Doctor's principles, as well as
writings. For the defence of truth, of law, and reafon, the Doctor's
book may be fafely confulted; but whoever wifhes to cheat a neighbour of his eftate, or to rob a country of its rights, need make no
fcruple of confulting the Doctor himfelf.

THE example of the Englifh nobility may, for aught I know, fufficiently juftify the Duke of Grafton, when he indulges his genius in
all the fafhionable exceffes of the age; yet, confidering his rank and
ftation, I think it would do him more honour to be able to deny the
fact, than to defend it by fuch authority. But if vice itfelf could be
excufed, there is yet a certain difplay of it, a certain outrage to decency, and violation of public decorum, which, for the benefit of fociety, fhould never be forgiven. It is not that he kept a miftrefs at
home, but that he conftantly attended her abroad. It is not the private indulgence, but the public infult, of which I complain. The
name of Mifs Parfons would hardly have been known, if the firft
lord of the treafury had not led her in triumph through the opera
houfe, even in the prefence of the Queen. When we fee a man act
in this manner, we may admit the fhamelefs depravity of his heart,
but what are we to think of his underftanding?

His Grace, it feems, is now to be a regular domeſtic man ; and as an omen of the future delicacy and correctneſs of his conduct, he marries a firſt couſin of the man who had fixed that mark and title of infamy upon him, which, at the ſame moment, makes a huſband unhappy and ridiculous. The ties of conſanguinity may poſſibly pre-ſerve him from the ſame fate a ſecond time ; and as to the diſtreſs of meeting, I take for granted the venerable uncle of theſe common cou-ſins has ſettled the etiquette in ſuch a manner, that, if a miſtake ſhould happen, it may reach no farther than from *Madame ma femme* to *Ma-dame ma couſine.*

The Duke of Grafton has always ſome excellent reaſon for deſert-ing his friends : The age and incapacity of Lord Chatham—the de-bility of Lord Rockingham—or the infamy of Mr. Wilkes. There was a time indeed when he did not appear to be quite ſo well ac-quainted, or ſo violently offended, with the infirmities of his friends. But now, I confeſs, they are not ill exchanged for the youthful vigo-rous virtue of the Duke of Bedford ; the firmneſs of General Con-way ; the blunt, or if I may call it the aukward, integrity of Mr. Rig-by ; and the ſpotleſs morality of Lord Sandwich.

If a late penſion to a broken gambler * be an act worthy of com-mendation, the Duke of Grafton's connexions will furniſh him with many opportunities of doing praiſe-worthy actions ; and as he him-ſelf bears no part of the expence, the generoſity of diſtributing the public money for the ſupport of virtuous families in diſtreſs will be an unqueſtionable proof of his Grace's humanity.

As to the public affairs, *Old Noll* is a little tender of deſcending to particulars. He does not deny that Corſica has been ſacrificed to France ; and he confeſſes, that, with regard to America, his patron's

---

* Sir John Moore

meafures have been fubject to fome variation ; but then he promifes
wonders of ftability and firmnefs for the future. Thefe are myfteries
of which we muft not pretend to judge by experience ; and truly, I
fear we fhall perifh in the defart, before we arrive at the land of promife. In the regular courfe of things, the period of the Duke of Grafton's minifterial manhood fhould now be approaching. The imbecillity of his infant-ftate was committed to Lord Chatham. Charles
Townfhend took fome care of his education at that ambiguous age
which lies between the follies of political childhood and the vices of
puberty. The empire of the paffions foon fucceeded. His earlieft
principles and connexions were of courfe forgotten or defpifed. The
company he has lately kept has been of no fervice to his morals ;
and, in the conduct of public affairs, we fee the character of his time
of life ftrongly diftinguifhed. An obftinate ungovernable felf-fuffi-
ciency plainly points out to us that ftate of imperfect maturity at
which the graceful levity of youth is loft, and the folidity of experience not yet acquired. It is poffible the young man may in time
grow wifer, and reform ; but, if I underftand his difpofition, it is not
of fuch corrigible ftuff, that we fhould hope for any amendment in
him, before he has accomplifhed the deftruction of this country. Like
other rakes, he may perhaps live to fee his error, but not until he has
ruined his eftate.

PHILO JUNIUS.

LETTER XV.

TO HIS GRACE THE DUKE OF GRAFTON.

MY LORD,   *JULY* 8. 1769.

IF nature had given you an underftanding qualified to keep pace
with the wifhes and principles of your heart, fhe would have made

you, perhaps, the moft formidable minifter that ever was employed, under a limited monarch, to accomplifh the ruin of a free people. When neither the feelings of fhame, the reproaches of confcience, nor the dread of punifhment, form any bar to the defigns of a mini- fter, the people would have too much reafon to lament their con- dition, if they did not find fome refource in the weaknefs of his underftanding. We owe it to the bounty of providence, that the completeft depravity of the heart is fometimes ftrangely united with a confufion of the mind, which counteracts the moft favourite prin- ciples, and makes the fame man treacherous without art, and a hy- pocrite without deceiving. The meafures, for inftance, in which your Grace's activity has been chiefly exerted, as they were adopted with- out fkill, fhould have been conducted with more than common dex- terity. But truly, my Lord, the execution has been as grofs as the defign. By one decifive ftep, you have defeated all the arts of wri- ting. You have fairly confounded the intrigues of oppofition, and filenced the clamours of faction. A dark ambiguous fyftem might require and furnifh the materials of ingenious illuftration ; and in doubtful meafures, the virulent exaggeration of party muft be em- ployed to roufe and engage the paffions of the people. You have now brought the merits of your adminiftration to an iffue, on which every Englifhman of the narroweft capacity may determine for him- felf. It is not an alarm to the paffions, but a calm appeal to the judg- ment of the people, upon their own moft effential interefts. A more experienced minifter would not have hazarded a direct invafion of the firft principles of the conftitution, before he had made fome pro- grefs in fubduing the fpirit of the people. With fuch a caufe as yours, my Lord, it is not fufficient that you have the court at your devo- tion, unlefs you can find means to corrupt or intimidate the jury.— The collective body of the people form that jury, and from *their* de- cifion there is but one appeal.

WHETHER you have talents to fupport you, at a crifis of fuch difficulty and danger, fhould long fince have been confidered. Judging truly of your difpofition, you have perhaps miftaken the extent of your capacity. Good-faith and folly have fo long been received as fynonymous terms, that the reverfe propofition has grown into credit, and every villain fancies himfelf a man of abilities. It is the apprehenfion of your friends, my Lord, that you have drawn fome hafty conclufion of this fort, and that a partial reliance upon your moral character has betrayed you beyond the depth of your underftanding. You have now carried things too far to retreat. You have plainly declared to the people what they are to expect from the continuance of your adminiftration. It is time for your Grace to confider what you alfo may expect in return from their fpirit and their refentment.

SINCE the acceffion of our moft gracious Sovereign to the throne, we have feen a fyftem of government which may well be called a reign of experiments. Parties of all denominations have been employed and difmiffed. The advice of the ableft men in this country has been repeatedly called for and rejected; and when the royal difpleafure has been fignified to a minifter, the marks of it have ufually been proportioned to his abilities and integrity. The fpirit of the FAVOURITE had fome apparent influence upon every adminiftration; and every fet of minifters preferved an appearance of duration as long as they fubmitted to that influence. But there were certain fervices to be performed for the favourite's fecurity, or to gratify his refentments, which your predeceffors in office had the wifdom or the virtue not to undertake. The moment this refractory fpirit was difcovered, their difgrace was determined. Lord Chatham, Mr. Grenville, and Lord Rockingham, have fucceffively had the honour to be difmiffed for preferring their duty, as fervants of the public, to thofe compliances which were expected from their ftation. A fubmiffive adminiftration was at laft gradually collected from the deferters of all parties, interefts, and connexions; and nothing remained but to find

L

a leader for thefe gallant well-difciplined troops. Stand forth, my
Lord, for thou art the man. Lord Bute found no refource of dependence or fecurity in the proud impofing fuperiority of Lord Chatham's abilities; the fhrewd inflexible judgment of Mr. Grenville;
nor in the mild but determined integrity of Lord Rockingham. His
views and fituation required a creature void of all thefe properties;
and he was forced to go through every divifion, refolution, compofition, and refinement of political chemiftry, before he happily arrived
at the *caput mortuum* of vitriol in your Grace. Flat and infipid in
your retired ftate, but brought into action you become vitriol again.
Such are the extremes of alternate indolence or fury which have governed your whole adminiftration. Your circumftances with regard
to the people foon becoming defperate, like other honeft fervants,
you determined to involve the beft of mafters in the fame difficulties
with yourfelf. We owe it to your Grace's well-directed labours, that
your Sovereign has been perfuaded to doubt of the affections of his
fubjects, and the people to fufpect the virtues of their Sovereign, at
a time when both were unqueftionable. You have degraded the royal
dignity into a bafe and difhonourable competition with Mr. Wilkes;
nor had you abilities to carry even the laft contemptible triumph
over a private man, without the groffeft violation of the fundamental laws of the conftitution and rights of the people. But thefe are
rights, my Lord, which you can no more annihilate than you can
the foil to which they are annexed. The queftion no longer turns
upon points of national honour and fecurity abroad, 'or on the degrees of expedience and propriety of meafures at home. It was not
inconfiftent that you fhould abandon the caufe of liberty in another
country, which you had perfecuted in your own; and in the common arts of domeftic corruption, we mifs no part of Sir Robert Walpole's fyftem, except his abilities. In this humble imitative line, you
might long have proceeded, fafe and contemptible: You might probably never have rifen to the dignity of being hated, and even have
been defpifed with moderation. But it feems you meant to be di-

ftinguifhed; and, to a mind like yours, there was no other road to fame but by the deftruction of a noble fabric, which you thought had been too long the admiration of mankind. The ufe you have made of the military force introduced an alarming change in the mode of executing the laws. The arbitrary appointment of Mr. Luttrell invades the foundation of the laws themfelves, as it manifeftly transfers the right of legiflation from thofe whom the people have chofen, to thofe whom they have rejected. With a fucceffion of fuch appointments, we may foon fee a Houfe of Commons collected, in the choice of which the other towns and counties of England will have as little fhare as the devoted county of Middlefex.

YET I truft that your Grace will find that the people of this country are neither to be intimidated by violent meafures, nor deceived by refinements. When they fee Mr. Luttrell feated in the Houfe of Commons, by mere dint of power, and in direct oppofition to the choice of a whole county, they will not liften to thofe fubtleties by which every arbitrary exertion of authority is explained into the law and privilege of parliament. It requires no perfuafion of argument, but fimply the evidence of the fenfes, to convince them, that, to tranf-fer the right of election from the collective to the reprefentative body of the people, contradicts all thofe ideas of a Houfe of Commons, which they have received from their forefathers, and which they had already, though vainly perhaps, delivered to their children. The principles on which this violent meafure has been defended have added fcorn to injury, and forced us to feel that we are not only oppreffed but infulted.

WITH what force, my Lord, with what protection, are you prepared to meet the united deteftation of the people of England? The city of London has given a generous example to the kingdom, in what manner a king of this country ought to be addreffed; and I fancy, my Lord, it is not yet in your courage to ftand between your

Sovereign and the addreffes of his fubjects. The injuries you have
done this country are fuch as demand not only redrefs but vengeance. In vain fhall you look for protection to that venal vote, which
you have already paid for—Another muft be purchafed ; and to fave
a minifter, the Houfe of Commons muft declare themfelves not only
independent of their conftituents, but the determined enemies of the
conftitution. Confider, my Lord, whether this be an extremity to
which their fears will permit them to advance ; or, if *their* protection fhould fail you, how far you are authorifed to rely upon the fincerity of thofe fmiles which a pious court-lavifhes without reluctance
upon a libertine by profeffion. It is not indeed the leaft of the thoufand contradictions which attend you, that a man, marked to the
world by the groffeft violation of all ceremony and decorum, fhould
be the firft fervant of a court, in which prayers are morality, and
kneeling is religion. Truft not too far to appearances, by which your
predeceffors have been deceived, though they have not been injured.
Even the beft of princes may at laft difcover, that this is a conten-
tion, in which every thing may be loft, but nothing can be gained ;
and as you became minifter by accident, were adopted without choice,
trufted without confidence, and continued without favour, be affured, that, whenever an occafion preffes, you will be difcarded without even the forms of regret. You will then have reafon to be thank-
ful, if you are permitted to retire to that feat of learning, which, in
contemplation of the fyftem of your life, the comparative purity of
your manners with thofe of their high fteward, and a thoufand other
recommending circumftances, has chofen you to encourage the grow-
ing virtue of their youth, and to prefide over their education. Whenever the fpirit of diftributing prebends and bifhopricks fhall have departed from you, you will find that learned feminary perfectly recovered from the delirium of an inftallation, and what in truth it ought
to be, once more a peaceful fcene of flumber and thoughtlefs meditation. The venerable tutors of the univerfity will no longer diftrefs
your modefty, by propofing you for a pattern to their pupils. The

learned dullnefs of declamation will be filent ; and even the venal
mufe, though happieft in fiction, will forget your virtues : Yet, for
the benefit of the fucceeding age, I could wifh that your retreat
might be deferred, until your morals fhall happily be ripened to that
maturity of corruption, at which the worft examples ceafe to be con-
tagious.

JUNIUS.

LETTER XVI.

TO THE PRINTER OF THE PUBLIC ADVERTISER.

SIR,   JULY 19. 1769.

A GREAT deal of ufelefs argument might have been faved in the
political conteft which has arifen from the expulfion of Mr. Wilkes,
and the fubfequent appointment of Mr. Luttrell, if the queftion had
been once ftated with precifion, to the fatisfaction of each party, and
clearly underftood by them both. But in this, as in almoft every other
difpute, it ufually happens, that much time is loft in referring to a multitude of cafes and precedents, which prove nothing to the purpofe ;
or in maintaining propofitions which are either not difputed, or,
whether they be admitted or denied, are entirely indifferent as to the
matter in debate ; until at laft the mind, perplexed and confounded
with the endlefs fubtleties of controverfy, lofes fight of the main
queftion, and never arrives at truth. Both parties in the difpute are
apt enough to practife thefe difhoneft artifices. The man who is confcious of the weaknefs of his caufe is interefted in concealing it ; and,
on the other fide, it is not uncommon to fee a good caufe mangled
by advocates who do not know the real ftrength of it.

I SHOULD be glad to know, for inftance, to what purpofe, in the

prefent cafe, fo many precedents have been produced to prove, That
the Houfe of Commons have a right to expel one of their own members ; that it belongs to them to judge of the validity of elections;
or, that the law of parliament is part of the law of the land ? * After
all thefe propofitions are admitted, Mr. Luttrell's right to his feat
will continue to be juft as difputable as it was before. Not one of
them is at prefent in agitation. Let it be admitted that the Houfe of
Commons were authorifed to expel Mr. Wilkes, that they are the
proper court to judge of elections, and that the law of parliament is
binding upon the people, ftill it remains to be inquired, whether the
Houfe, by their refolution in favour of Mr. Luttrell, have or have
not truly declared that law. To facilitate this inquiry, I would have
the queftion cleared of all foreign or indifferent matter. The following ftate of it will probably be thought a fair one by both parties ;
and then I imagine there is no gentleman in this country, who will
not be capable of forming a judicious and true opinion upon it. I
take the queftion to be ftrictly this—" Whether or no it be the known
eftablifhed law of parliament, that the expulfion of a member of the
Houfe of Commons of itfelf creates in him fuch an incapacity to be
re-elected, that, at a fubfequent election, any votes given to him are
null and void ; and that any other candidate who, except the perfon
expelled, has the greateft number of votes, ought to be the fitting
member ?"

To prove that the affirmative is the law of parliament, I apprehend
it is not fufficient for the prefent Houfe of Commons to declare it to
be fo. We may fhut our eyes indeed to the dangerous confequences
of fuffering one branch of the legiflature to declare new laws, without argument or example, and it may perhaps be prudent enough to
fubmit to authority ; but a mere affertion will never convince, much

---

* The reader will obferve, that thefe admiffions are made, not as of truths unqueftionable, but for the
fake of argument, and in order to bring the real queftion to iffue.

fefs will it be thought reafonable to prove the right by the fact itfelf. The miniftry have not yet pretended to fuch a tyranny over our minds. To fupport the affirmative fairly, it will either be neceffary to produce fome ftatute in which that pofitive provifion fhall have been made, that fpecific difability clearly created, and the confequences of it declared; or, if there be no fuch ftatute, the cuftom of parliament muft then be referred to; and fome cafe or cafes * ftrictly in point muft be produced, with the decifion of the court upon them; for I readily admit, that the cuftom of parliament, once clearly proved, is equally binding with the common and ftatute law.

THE confideration of what may be reafonable or unreafonable makes no part of this queftion. We are inquiring what the law is, not what it ought to be. Reafon may be applied to fhow the impropriety or expedience of a law, but we muft have either ftatute or precedent to prove the exiftence of it. At the fame time I do not mean to admit that the late refolution of the Houfe of Commons is defenfible on general principles of reafon any more than in law.— This is not the hinge on which the debate turns.

SUPPOSING therefore that I have laid down an accurate ftate of the queftion, I will venture to affirm, 1ft, That there is no ftatute exifting by which that fpecific difability which we fpeak of is created. If there be, let it be produced. The argument will then be at an end.

2dly, That there is no precedent in all the proceedings of the Houfe of Commons, which comes entirely home to the prefent cafe, viz. " Where an expelled member has been returned again, and another candidate, with an inferior number of votes, has been declared

---

* Precedents, in oppofition to principles, have little weight with *Junius*; but he thought it neceffary to meet the miniftry upon their own ground.

the fitting member." If there be fuch a precedent, let it be given to us plainly, and I am fure it will have more weight than all the cunning arguments which have been drawn from inferences and probabilities.

THE miniftry, in that laborious pamphlet which I prefume contains the whole ftrength of the party, have declared *, " That Mr. Walpole's was the firft and only inftance in which the electors of any county or borough had returned a perfon expelled to ferve in the fame parliament." It is not poffible to conceive a cafe more exactly in point. Mr. Walpole was expelled ; and, having a majority of votes at the next election, was returned again. The friends of Mr. Taylor, a candidate fet up by the miniftry, petitioned the Houfe that he might be the fitting member. Thus far the circumftances tally exactly, except that our Houfe of Commons faved Mr. Luttrell the trouble of petitioning. The point of law, however, was the fame. It came regularly before the Houfe, and it was their bufinefs to determine upon it. They did determine it, for they declared Mr. Taylor *not duly elected.* If it be faid that they meant this refolution as matter of favour and indulgence to the borough which had retorted Mr. Walpole upon them, in order that the burgeffes, knowing what the law was, might correct their error, I anfwer—

I. THAT it is a ftrange way of arguing to oppofe a fuppofition, which no man can prove, to a fact which proves itfelf.

II. THAT, if this were the intention of the Houfe of Commons, it muft have defeated itfelf. The burgeffes of Lynn could never have known their error, much lefs could they have corrected it by any inftruction they received from the proceedings of the Houfe of Commons. They might perhaps have forefeen, that, if they returned Mr.

---

* *Cafe of the Middlefex election confidered.* page 38.

Walpole again, he would again be rejected ; but they never could infer, from a resolution by which the candidate with the fewest votes was declared *not duly elected*, that, at a future election, and in similar circumstances, the House of Commons would reverse their resolution, and receive the same candidate as duly elected, whom they had before rejected.

THIS indeed would have been a most extraordinary way of declaring the law of parliament, and what I presume no man, whose understanding is not at cross-purposes with itself, could possibly understand.

IF, in a case of this importance, I thought myself at liberty to argue from suppositions rather than from facts, I think the probability in this instance is directly the reverse of what the ministry affirm ; and that it is much more likely that the House of Commons at that time would rather have strained a point in favour of Mr. Taylor, than that they would have violated the law of parliament, and robbed Mr. Taylor of a right legally vested in him to gratify a refractory borough, which, in defiance of them, had returned a person branded with the strongest mark of the displeasure of the House.

BUT really, Sir, this way of talking, for I cannot call it argument, is a mockery of the common understanding of the nation too gross to be endured. Our dearest interests are at stake. An attempt has been made, not merely to rob a single county of its rights, but, by inevitable consequence, to alter the constitution of the House of Commons. This fatal attempt has succeeded, and stands as a precedent recorded for ever. If the ministry are unable to defend their cause by fair argument founded on facts, let them spare us at least the mortification of being amused and deluded like children. I believe there is yet a spirit of resistance in this country which will not submit to

M.

be oppreffed; but I am fure there is a fund of good fenfe in this country which cannot be deceived.

JUNIUS.

LETTER XVII.

TO THE PRINTER OF THE PUBLIC ADVERTISER.

SIR,   —   AUGUST 1. 1769.

IT will not be neceffary for *Junius* to take the trouble of anfwering your correfpondent G. A. or the quotation from a fpeech without doors, publifhed in your paper of the 28th of laft month. The fpeech appeared before *Junius's* letter; and as the author feems to confider the great propofition, on which all his arguments depend, viz. *that Mr. Wilkes was under that known legal incapacity of which Junius fpeaks*, as a point granted, his fpeech is in no fhape an anfwer to *Junius*, for this is the very queftion in debate.

As to G. A. I obferve, firft, that if he did not admit *Junius's* ftate of the queftion, he fhould have fhown the fallacy of it, or given us a more exact one;—fecondly, that, confidering the many hours and days which the miniftry and their advocates have wafted, in public debate, in compiling large quartos, and collecting innumerable pre-cedents, exprefsly to prove, that the late proceedings of the Houfe of Commons are warranted by the law, cuftom, and practice of par-liament, it is rather an extraordinary fuppofition, to be made by one of their own party even for the fake of argument, *that no fuch ftatute, no fuch cuftom of parliament, no fuch cafe in point, can be produced.*—G. A. may however make the fuppofition with fafety. It contains nothing, but literally the fact, except that there is a cafe exactly in point, with a decifion of the Houfe diametrically oppofite to that which the prefent Houfe of Commons came to in favour of Mr. Luttrell.

THE miniftry now begin to be afhamed of the weaknefs of their caufe; and, as it ufually happens with falfehood, are driven to the neceffity of fhifting their ground, and changing their whole defence. At firft we were told, that nothing could be clearer than that the proceedings of the Houfe of Commons were juftified by the known law and uniform cuftom of parliament. But now it feems, if there be no law, the Houfe of Commons have a right to make one; and if there be no precedent, they have a right to create the firft: For this I prefume is the amount of the queftions propofed to *Junius*. If your correfpondent had been at all verfed in the law of parliament, or generally in the laws of this country, he would have feen. that this defence is as weak and falfe as the former.

THE privileges of either houfe of parliament, it is true, are inde-finite, that is, they have not been defcribed or laid down in any one code or declaration whatfoever; but whenever a queftion of privilege has arifen, it has invariably been difputed or maintained upon the footing of precedents alone *. In the courfe of the proceedings upon. the Aylefbury election, the Houfe of Lords refolved, "That neither houfe of parliament had any power, by any vote or declaration, to create to themfelves any new privilege that was not warranted by the known laws and cuftoms of parliament." And to this rule the Houfe of Commons, though otherwife they had acted in a very arbitrary manner, gave their affent; for they affirmed that they had guided themfelves by it, in afferting their privileges. Now, Sir, if this be true with refpect to matters of privilege, in which the Houfe.

---

* This is ftill meeting the miniftry upon their own ground; for, in truth, no precedents will fupport: either natural injuftice, or violation of pofitive right.

M. 2.

of Commons, individually and as a body, are principally concerned, how much more ftrongly will it hold againft any pretended power in that Houfe to create or declare a new law, by which not only the rights of the Houfe over their own member, and thofe of the member himfelf, are included, but alfo thofe of a third and feparate party, I mean the freeholders of the kingdom. To do juftice to the miniftry, they have not yet pretended that any one or any two of the three eftates have power to make a new law, without the concurrence of the third. They know that a man who maintains fuch a doctrine is liable, by ftatute, to the heavieft penalties. They do not acknowledge that the Houfe of Commons have affumed a *new* privilege, or declared a *new* law. On the contrary, they affirm, that their proceedings have been ftrictly conformable to and founded upon the ancient law and cuftom of parliament. Thus therefore the queftion returns to the point at which *Junius* had fixed it, viz. *Whether or no this be the law of parliament.* If it be not, the Houfe of Commons had no legal authority to eftablifh the precedent; and the precedent itfelf is a mere fact, without any proof of right whatfoever.

YOUR correfpondent concludes with a queftion of the fimpleft nature: *Muſt a thing be wrong, becauſe it has never been done before?* No. But, admitting it were proper to be done, that alone does not convey an authority to do it. As to the prefent cafe, I hope I fhall never fee the time, when not only a fingle perfon, but a whole county, and in effect the entire collective body of the people, may again be robbed of their birth-right by a vote of the Houfe of Commons. But if, for reafons which I am unable to comprehend, it be neceffary to truft that Houfe with a power fo exorbitant and fo unconftitutional, at leaft let it be given to them by an act of the legiflature.

PHILO JUNIUS.

LETTER XVIII.

TO SIR WILLIAM BLACKSTONE, SOLICITOR GENERAL TO HER MAJESTY.

SIR,   *JULY* 29. 1769.

I SHALL make you no apology for confidering a certain pamphlet, in which your late conduct is defended, as written by yourfelf. The perfonal intereft, the perfonal refentments, and above all that wounded fpirit, unaccuftomed to reproach, and I hope not frequently confcious of deferving it, are fignals which betray the author to us as plainly as if your name were in the title-page. You appeal to the public in defence of your reputation. We hold it, Sir, that an injury offered to an individual is interefting to fociety. On this principle the people of England made common caufe with Mr. Wilkes. On this principle, if *you* are injured, they will join in your refentment. I fhall not follow you through the infipid form of a third perfon, but addrefs myfelf to you directly.

YOU feem to think the channel of a pamphlet more refpectable, and better fuited to the dignity of your caufe, than that of a newfpaper. Be it fo. Yet if newfpapers are fcurrilous, you muft confefs they are impartial. They give us, without any apparent preference, the wit and argument of the miniftry, as well as the abufive dulnefs of the oppofition. The fcales are equally poifed. It is not the printer's fault if the greater weight inclines the balance.

YOUR pamphlet then is divided into an attack upon Mr. Grenville's character and a defence of your own. It would have been more confiftent perhaps with your profeffed intention, to have confined yourfelf to the laft. But anger has fome claim to indulgence,

and railing is ufually a relief to the mind. I hope you have found
benefit from the experiment. It is not my defign to enter into a formal vindication of Mr. Grenville, upon his own principles. I have
neither the honour of being perfonally known to him, nor do I pretend to be completely mafter of all the facts. I need not run the rifk
of doing an injuftice to his opinions, or to his conduct, when your
pamphlet alone carries, upon the face of it, a full vindication of both...

YOUR firft reflection is, that Mr. Grenville * was, of all men, the
perfon who fhould not have complained of inconfiftence with regard
to Mr. Wilkes. This, Sir, is either an unmeaning fneer, a peevifh
expreffion of refentment, or, if it means any thing, you plainly beg
the queftion ; for whether his parliamentary conduct with regard to
Mr. Wilkes has or has not been inconfiftent, remains yet to be proved. But it feems he received upon the fpot a fufficient chaftifement
for exercifing *fo unfairly* his talents of mifreprefentation. You are a
lawyer, Sir, and know better than I do upon what particular occafions a talent for mifreprefentation may be *fairly* exerted ; but to punifh a man a fecond time, when he has been once fufficiently chafti-
fed, is rather too fevere. It is not in the laws of England ; it is not
in your own commentaries ; nor is it yet, I believe, in the new law
you have revealed to the Houfe of Commons. I hope this doctrine
has no exiftence but in your own heart. After all, Sir, if you had
confulted that fober difcretion, which you feem to oppofe with triumph to the honeft jollity of a tavern, it might have occurred to
you, that, although you could have fucceeded in fixing a charge of
inconfiftence upon Mr. Grenville, it would not have tended in any
fhape to exculpate yourfelf.

YOUR next infinuation, that Sir William Meredith had haftily

* Mr. Grenville had quoted a paffage from the Doctor's excellent commentaries, which directly contradicted the doctrine maintained by the Doctor in the Houfe of Commons.

adopted the falfe gloffes of his new ally, is of the fame fort with the firft. It conveys a fneer as little worthy of the gravity of your character, as it is ufelefs to your defence. It is of little moment to the public to inquire, by whom the charge was conceived, or by whom it was adopted? The only queftion we afk is, Whether or no it be true? The remainder of your reflections upon Mr. Grenville's conduct deftroy themfelves. He could not poffibly come prepared to traduce your integrity to the Houfe. He could not forefee that you would even fpeak upon the queftion; much lefs could he forefee that you would maintain a direct contradiction of that doctrine which you had folemnly, difintereftedly, and upon fobereft reflection, delivered to the public. He came armed indeed with what he thought a refpectable authority, to fupport what he was convinced was the caufe of truth; and I doubt not he intended to give you, in the courfe of the debate, an honourable and public teftimony of his efteem.— Thinking highly of his abilities, I cannot however allow him the gift of divination. As to what you are pleafed to call a plan coolly formed to impofe upon the Houfe of Commons, and his producing it without provocation at midnight, I confider it as the language of pique and invective, therefore unworthy of regard. But, Sir, I am fenfible I have followed your example too long, and wandered from the point.

THE quotation from your commentaries is matter of record. It can neither be *altered* by your friends, nor mifreprefented by your enemies; and I am willing to take your own word for what you have faid in the Houfe of Commons. If there be a real difference between what you have written and what you have fpoken, you confefs that your book ought to be the ftandard. Now, Sir, if words mean any thing, I apprehend, that, when a long enumeration of difqualifications (whether by ftatute or the cuftom of parliament) concludes with thefe general comprehenfive words, " But, fubject to thefe reftrictions and difqualifications, *every* fubject of the realm is eligible of common right," a reader of plain underftanding muft of courfe reft fatisfied that no fpecies of difqualification whatfoever had been omitted. The known character of the author, and the apparent accuracy with which the whole work is compiled, would confirm him in his opinion; nor could he poffibly form any other judgment, without looking upon your commentaries in the fame light in which you confider thofe penal laws which, though not repealed, are fallen into difufe, and are now in effect A SNARE TO THE UNWARY *.

You tell us indeed that it was not part of your plan to fpecify any temporary incapacity.; and that you could not, without a fpirit of prophecy, have fpecified the difability of a private individual, fubfequent to the period at which you wrote. What your plan was, I know not; but what it fhould have been, in order to complete the work you have given us, is by no means difficult to determine. The incapacity, which you call temporary, may continue feven years; and though you might not have forefeen the particular cafe of Mr. Wilkes, you might and fhould have forefeen the poffibility of *fuch* a cafe, and told us how far the Houfe of Commons were authorifed to proceed in it by the law and cuftom of parliament. The freeholders of Middlefex would then have known what they had to truft to, and would never have returned Mr. Wilkes, when Colonel Luttrell was a candidate againft him. They would have chofen fome indifferent perfon, rather than fubmit to be reprefented by the object of their contempt and deteftation.

Your attempt to diftinguifh between difabilities which affect whole claffes of men, and thofe which affect individuals only, is really unworthy of your underftanding. Your commentaries had taught me,

---

* If, in ftating the law upon any point, a judge deliberately affirms that he has included *every* cafe, and it fhould appear that he has purpofely omitted a material cafe, he does in effect lay a fnare for the unwary.

that, although the inftance in which a penal law is exerted be particular, the laws themfelves are general. They are made for the benefit and inftruction of the public, though the penalty falls only upon
an individual. You cannot but know, Sir, that what was Mr. Wilkes's
cafe yefterday may be your's or mine to-morrow, and that confequently the common right of every fubject of the realm is invaded
by it. Profefling therefore to treat of the conftitution of the Houfe
of Commons, and of the laws and cuftoms relative to that conftitution, you certainly were guilty of a moft unpardonable omiffion in
taking no notice of a right and privilege of the Houfe, more extraordinary and more arbitrary than all the others they poffefs put together. If the expulfion of a member, not under any legal difability,
of itfelf creates in him an incapacity to be elected, I fee a ready way
marked out, by which the majority may at any time remove the ho-
nefteft and ableft men who happen to be in oppofition to them.
To fay that they *will not* make this extravagant ufe of their power,
would be a language unfit for a man fo learned in the laws as you
are. By your doctrine, Sir, they *have* the power; and laws, you
know, are intended to guard againft what men *may* do, not to truft
to what they *will* do.

UPON the whole, Sir, the charge againft you is of a plain fimple
nature : It appears even upon the face of your own pamphlet. On
the contrary, your juftification of yourfelf is full of fubtlety and refinement, and in fome places not very intelligible. If I were perfonally your enemy, I fhould dwell, with a malignant pleafure, upon
thofe great and ufeful qualifications which you certainly poffefs, and
by which you once acquired, though they could not preferve to you,
the refpect and efteem of your country. I fhould enumerate the honours you have loft, and the virtues you have difgraced : But having
no private refentments to gratify, I think it fufficient to have given
my opinion of your public conduct, leaving the punifhment it deferves to your clofet and to yourfelf.   J U N I U S.

N

LETTER XIX.

SIR,   *AUGUST 14. 1769.*

A CORRESPONDENT of the St. James's Evening Poſt firſt wilfully mifunderſtands Junius, then cenſures him for a bad reaſoner. Junius does not ſay that it was incumbent upon Dr. Blackſtone to foreſee and ſtate the crimes for which Mr. Wilkes was expelled. If, by a ſpirit of prophecy, he had even done ſo, it would have been nothing to the purpoſe. The queſtion is, not for what particular offences a perſon may be expelled; but generally whether by the law of parliament expulſion alone creates a diſqualifieation. If the affirmative be the law of parliament, Dr. Blackſtone might and ſhould have told us ſo. The queſtion is not confined to this or that particular perſon, but forms one great general branch of diſqualification, too important in itſelf, and too extenſive in its conſequences, to be omitted in an accurate work expreſsly treating of the law of parliament.

THE truth of the matter is evidently this. Dr. Blackſtone, while he was ſpeaking in the Houſe of Commons, never once thought of his commentaries, until the contradiction was unexpectedly urged, and ſtared him in the face. Inſtead of defending himſelf upon the ſpot, he ſunk under the charge, in an agony of confuſion and deſpair. It is well known that there was a pauſe of ſome minutes in the Houſe, from a general expectation that the Doctor would ſay ſomething in his own defence ; but it ſeems his faculties were too much overpowered to think of thoſe ſubtleties and refinements which have ſince occurred to him. It was then Mr. Grenville received the ſevere chaſtiſement, which the Doctor mentions with ſo much triumph. *I wiſh the honourable gentleman, inſtead of ſhaking his head, would fhake a good argument out of it.* If to the elegance, novelty, and bitternefs of this ingenious farcdfm, we add the natural melody of the amiable Sir Fletcher Norton's pipe, we fhall not be furprifed that Mr. Grenville was unable to make him any reply.

As to the Doctor, I would recommend it to him to be quiet. If not, he may perhaps hear again from Junius himfelf.

PHILO JUNIUS.

POSTSCRIPT TO A PAMPHLET INTITLED,

' *An Anfwer to the Queftion ftated.*'

Suppofed to be written by Dr. Blackftone, Solicitor to the Queen, in Anfwer to Junius's Letter.

SINCE thefe papers were fent to the prefs, a writer in the public papers, who fubfcribes himfelf Junius, has made a feint of bringing this queftion to a fhort iffue. Though the foregoing obfervations contain, in my opinion at leaft, a full refutation of all that this writer has offered, I fhall however beftow a very few words upon him. It will coft me very little trouble to unravel and expofe the fophiftry of his argument.

" I TAKE the queftion (fays he) to be ftrictly this : Whether or no it be the known eftablifhed law of parliament, that the expulfion of a member of the Houfe of Commons of itfelf creates in him fuch an incapacity to be re-elected, that, at a fubfequent election, any votes given to him are null and void ; and that any other candidate, who, except the perfon expelled, has the greateft number of votes, ought to be the fitting member."

N 2

WAVING for the prefent any objection I may have to this ftate of the queftion, I fhall venture to meet our champion upon his own ground; and attempt to fupport the affirmative of it, in one of the two ways by which he fays it can be alone fairly fupported.—" If there be no ftatute (fays he) in which the fpecific difability is clearly created, &c. (and we acknowledge there is none), the cuftom of parliament muft then be referred to, and fome cafe or cafes, ftrictly in point, muft be produced, with the decifion of the court upon them." Now I affert, that this has been done. Mr. Walpole's cafe is ftrictly in point, to prove, that expulfion creates abfolute incapacity of being re-elected. This was the clear decifion of the Houfe upon it; and was a full declaration that incapacity was the neceffary confequence of expulfion. The law was as clearly and firmly fixed by this refolution, and is as binding in every fubfequent cafe of expulfion, as if it had been declared by an exprefs ftatute, "that a member expelled by a refolution of the Houfe of Commons fhall be deemed incapable of being re-elected." Whatever doubt then there might have been of the law before Mr. Walpole's cafe, with refpect to the full operation of a vote of expulfion, there can be none now. The decifion of the Houfe upon this cafe is ftrictly in point to prove, that expulfion creates abfolute incapacity in law of being re-elected.

BUT incapacity in law in this inftance muft have the fame operation and effect with incapacity in law in every other inftance. Now, incapacity of being re-elected implies in its very terms, that any votes given to the incapable perfon at a fubfequent election are null and void. This is its neceffary operation, or it has no operation at all: It is *vox et praeterea nihil.* We can no more be called upon to prove this propofition than we can to prove that a dead man is not alive, or that twice two are four. When the terms are underftood, the propofition is felf-evident.

LASTLY, it is, in all cafes of election, the known and eftablifhed law of the land, grounded upon the cleareſt principles of reaſon and common ſenſe, that, if the votes given to one candidate are null and void, they cannot be oppoſed to the votes given to another candidate: They cannot affect the votes of ſuch candidate at all. As they have on the one hand no poſitive quality to add or eſtabliſh, ſo have they on the other hand no negative one to ſubtract or deſtroy. They are, in a word, a mere non-entity. Such was the determination of the Houſe of Commons in the Malden and Bedford elections; caſes ſtrictly in point to the preſent queſtion, as far as they are meant to be in point. And to ſay that they are not in point in all circumſtances, in thoſe particularly which are independent of the propoſition which they are quoted to prove, is to ſay no more than that Malden is not Middleſex, nor Serjeant Comyns Mr. Wilkes.

LET us ſee then how our proof ſtands. Expulſion creates incapacity, incapacity annihilates any votes given to the incapable perſon; the votes given to the qualified candidate ſtand upon their own bottom, firm and untouched, and can alone have effect. This, one would think, would be ſufficient. But we are ſtopped ſhort, and told, that none of our precedents come home to the preſent caſe; and are challenged to produce " a precedent in all the proceedings of the Houſe of Commons that does come home to it, viz. *where an expelled member has been returned again, and another candidate, with an inferior number of votes, has been declared the ſitting member.*"

INSTEAD of a precedent, I will beg leave to put a caſe, which, I fancy, will be quite as deciſive to the preſent point. Suppoſe another Sachaverel (and every party muſt have its Sachaverel) ſhould, at ſome future election, take it into his head to offer himſelf a candidate for the county of Middleſex: He is oppoſed by a candidate, whoſe coat is of a different colour; but, however, of a very good colour. The divine has an indiſputable majority; nay, the poor layman is abſolutely diſtanced. The ſheriff, after having had his conſcience well

informed by the reverend cafuift, returns him, as he fuppofes, duly
elected. The whole Houfe is in an uproar at the apprehenfion of fo
ftrange an appearance amongft them. A motion however is at length
made, that the perfon was incapable of being elected, that his election therefore is null and void, and that his competitor ought to have
been returned. No, fays a great orator, firft fhow me your law for
this proceeding. " Either produce me a ftatute in which the fpecific
difability of a clergyman is created, or produce me a precedent *where
a clergyman has been returned, and another candidate, with an inferior
number of votes, has been declared the fitting member."* No fuch ftatute, no fuch precedent, to be found. What anfwer then is to be given to this demand? The very fame anfwer which I will give to that
of Junius : That there is more than one precedent in the proceedings
of the Houfe—" where an incapable perfon has been returned, and
another candidate, with an inferior number of votes, has been declared the fitting member ; and that this is the known and eftablifhed law in all cafes of incapacity, from whatever caufe it may arife."

I SHALL now therefore beg leave to make a flight amendment to
Junius's ftate of the queftion, the affirmative of which will then ftand
thus :

" IT is the known and eftablifhed law of parliament, that the expulfion of any member of the Houfe of Commons creates in him an
incapacity of being re-elected ; that any votes given to him at a fubfequent election are, in confequence of fuch incapacity, null and
void ; and that any other candidate who, except the perfon rendered incapable, has the greateft number of votes, ought to be the fitting
member."

BUT our bufinefs is not yet quite finifhed. Mr. Walpole's cafe
muft have a re-hearing. " It is not poffible (fays this writer) to conceive a cafe more exactly in point. Mr. Walpole was expelled ; and

having a majority of votes at the next election was returned again. The friends of Mr. Taylor, a candidate set up by the miniftry, petitioned the Houfe that he might be the fitting member. Thus far the circumftances tally exactly, except that our Houfe of Commons faved Mr. Luttrell the trouble of petitioning. The point of law, however, was the fame. It came regularly before the Houfe, and it was their bufinefs to determine upon it. They did determine it; for they declared Mr. Taylor *not duly elected*."

INSTEAD of examining the juftnefs of this reprefentation, I fhall beg leave to oppofe againft it my own view of this cafe, in as plain a manner and as few words as I am able.

IT was the known and eftablifhed law of parliament, when the charge againft Mr. Walpole came before the Houfe of Commons, that they had power to expel, to difable, and to render incapable for offences. In virtue of this power they expelled him.

HAD they, in the very vote of expulfion, adjudging him, in terms, to be incapable of being re-elected, there muft have been at once an end with him. But though the right of the Houfe, both to expel and adjudge incapable, was clear and indubitable, it does not appear to me, that the full operation and effect of a vote of expulfion fingly was fo.—The law in this cafe had never been exprefsly declared.— There had been no event to call up fuch a declaration. I trouble not myfelf with the grammatical meaning of the word expulfion, I regard only its legal meaning. This was not, as I think, precifely fixed. The Houfe thought proper to fix it, and explicitly to declare the full confequences of their former vote, before they fuffered thefe confequences to take effect. And in this proceeding they acted upon the moft liberal and folid principles of equity, juftice, and law. What then did the burgeffes of Lynn collect from the fecond vote? Their fubfequent conduct will tell us: It will with certainty tell us, that they confidered it as decifive againft Mr. Walpole; it will alfo with equal certainty tell us, that, upon fuppofition that the law of election ftood then as it does now, and that they knew it to ftand thus, they inferred, " that, at a future election, and in cafe of a fimilar return, the Houfe would receive the fame candidate, as duly elected, whom they had before rejected." They could infer nothing but this.

It is needlefs to repeat the circumftance of diffimilarity in the prefent cafe. It will be fufficient to obferve, that, as the law of parliament, upon which the Houfe of Commons grounded every ftep of their proceedings, was clear beyond the reach of doubt, fo neither could the freeholders of Middlefex be at a lofs to forefee what muft be the inevitable confequence of their proceedings in oppofition to it. For upon every return of Mr. Wilkes, the Houfe made inquiry whether any votes were given to any other candidate.

But I could venture, for the experiment's fake, even to give this writer the utmoft he afks; to allow the moft perfect fimilarity throughout in thefe two cafes; to allow, that the law of expulfion was quite as clear to the burgeffes of Lynn, as to the freeholders of Middlefex. It will, I am confident, avail his caufe but little. It will only prove, that the law of election at that time was different from the prefent law. It will prove, that, in all cafes of an incapable candidate returned, the law then was, that the whole election fhould be void. But now we know that this is not law. The cafes of Malden and Bedford were, as has been feen, determined upon other and more juft principles. And thefe determinations are, I imagine, admitted on all fides to be law.

I would willingly draw a veil over the remaining part of this paper. It is aftonifhing, it is painful, to fee men of parts and ability, giving into the moft unworthy artifices, and defcending fo much below their true line of character. But if they are not the dupes of their fophiftry (which is hardly to be conceived), let them confider that they are fomething much worfe.

THE deareft interefts of this country are its laws and its conftitution. Againft every attack upon thefe, there will, I hope, be always found amongft us the firmeft *fpirit of refiftance;* fuperior to the united efforts of faction and ambition. For ambition, though it does not always take the lead of faction, will be fure in the end to make the moft fatal advantage of it, and draw it to its own purpofes. But I truft our day of trial is yet far off; and there is *a fund of good fenfe in this country, which cannot long be deceived* by the arts either of falfe reafoning or falfe patriotifm.

LETTER XX.

TO THE PRINTER OF THE PUBLIC ADVERTISER.

SIR,   *AUGUST* 8. 1769.

THE gentleman who has publifhed an anfwer to Sir William Meredith's pamphlet, having honoured me with a poftfcript of fix quarto pages, which he moderately calls beftowing a *very* few words upon me, I cannot, in common politenefs, refufe him a reply. The form and magnitude of a quarto impofes upon the mind; and men, who are unequal to the labour of difcuffing an intricate argument, or wifh to avoid it, are willing enough to fuppofe, that much has been proved, becaufe much has been faid. Mine, I confefs, are humble labours. I do not prefume to inftruct the learned, but fimply to inform the body of the people; and I prefer that channel of conveyance which is likely to fpread fartheft among them. The advocates of the miniftry feem to me to write for fame, and to flatter them-

O

felves that the fize of their works will make them immortal. They
pile up reluctant quarto upon folid folio, as if their labours, becaufe
they are gigantic, could contend with truth and heaven.

THE writer of the volume in queftion meets me upon my own
ground. He acknowledges there is no ftatute by which the fpecific
difability we fpeak of is created; but he affirms that the cuftom of
parliament has been referred to, and that a cafe ftrictly in point has
been produced, with the decifion of the court upon it. I thank him
for coming fo fairly to the point. He afferts that the cafe of Mr.
Walpole is ftrictly in point to prove, that expulfion creates an abfolute incapacity of being re-elected; and for this purpofe he refers generally to the firft vote of the Houfe upon that occafion, without
venturing to recite the vote itfelf. The unfair difingenuous artifice of
adopting that part of a precedent which feems to fuit his purpofe,
and omitting the remainder, deferves fome pity, but cannot excite my
refentment. He takes advantage eagerly of the firft refolution, by
which Mr. Walpole's incapacity is declared; but as to the two following, by which the candidate with the feweft votes was declared
" not duly elected," and the election itfelf vacated, I dare fay he
would be well fatisfied if they were for ever blotted out of the journals of the Houfe of Commons. In fair argument, no part of a precedent fhould be admitted, unlefs the whole of it be given to us together. The author has divided his precedent; for he knew, that,
taken together, it produced a confequence directly the reverfe of that
which he endeavours to draw from a vote of expulfion. But what
will this honeft perfon fay, if I take him at his word, and demon-
ftrate to him, that the Houfe of Commons never meant to found Mr.
Walpole's incapacity upon his expulfion only? what fubterfuge will
then remain?

LET it be remembered, that we are fpeaking of the intention of
men who lived more than half a century ago, and that fuch intention

can only be collected from their words and actions as they are delivered to us upon record. To prove their designs by a supposition of
what they would have done, opposed to what they actually did, is
mere trifling and impertinence. The vote by which Mr. Walpole's
incapacity was declared is thus expressed, "That Robert Walpole,
Esq. having been this session of parliament committed a prisoner to
the Tower, and expelled this House for a breach of trust in the execution of his office, and notorious corruption when secretary at war,
was and is incapable of being elected a member to serve in this present parliament *."—Now, Sir, to my understanding, no proposition
of this kind can be more evident, than that the House of Commons,
by this very vote, themselves understood, and meant to declare, that
Mr. Walpole's incapacity arose from the crimes he had committed,
not from the punishment the House annexed to them. The high
breach of trust, the notorious corruption, are stated in the strongest
terms. They do not tell us that he was incapable because he was expelled, but because he had been guilty of such offences as justly rendered him unworthy of a seat in parliament. If they had intended
to fix the disability upon his expulsion alone, the mention of his
crimes in the same vote would have been highly improper. It could
only perplex the minds of the electors, who, if they collected any
thing from so confused a declaration of the law of parliament, must
have concluded that their representative had been declared incapable
because he was highly guilty, not because he had been punished.—
But even admitting them to have understood it in the other sense,
they must then, from the very terms of the vote, have united the

---

* It is well worth remarking, that the compiler of a certain quarto, called, *The case of the last election for the county of Middlesex considered,* has the impudence to recite this very vote, in the following terms, vide p. 11. "Resolved, that Robert Walpole, Esq. having been that session of parliament expelled the House, was and is incapable of being elected a member to serve in the present parliament." There cannot be a stronger positive proof of the treachery of the compiler, nor a stronger presumptive proof that he was convinced that the vote, if truly recited, would overturn his whole argument.

idea of his being sent to the Tower with that of his expulsion, and considered his incapacity as the joint effect of both *.

* ADDRESSED TO THE PRINTER OF THE PUBLIC ADVERTISER.

SIR,   MAY 22. 1771.

VERY early in the debate upon the decision of the Middlesex election, it was observed by *Junius*, that the House of Commons had not only exceeded their boasted precedent of the expulsion and subsequent incapacitation of Mr. Walpole, but that they had not even adhered to it strictly as far as it went. After convicting Mr. Dyson of giving a false quotation from the journals, and having explained the purpose which that contemptible fraud was intended to answer, he proceeds to state the vote itself by which Mr. Walpole's supposed incapacity was declared, viz.—" Resolved, That Robert Walpole, Esq. having been this session of parliament committed a prisoner to the Tower, and expelled this house for a high breach of trust in the execution of his office, and notorious corruption when secretary at war, was and is incapable of being elected a member to serve in this present parliament :"—and then observes, that, from the terms of the vote, we have no right to annex the incapacitation to the *expulsion* only; for that, as the proposition stands, it must arise equally from the expulsion and the commitment to the Tower. I believe, Sir, no man, who knows any thing of Dialectics, or who understands English, will dispute the truth and fairness of this construction. But *Junius* has a great authority to support him, which, to speak with the Duke of Grafton, I accidentally met with this morning in the course of my reading. It contains an admonition, which cannot be repeated too often. Lord Sommers, in his excellent tract upon the rights of the people, after reciting the votes of the convention of the 28th of January 1689, viz.—" That King James the Second, having endeavoured to subvert the constitution of this kingdom by breaking the original contract between King and people, and by the advice of Jesuits and other wicked persons having violated the fundamental laws, and having withdrawn himself out of this kingdom, hath abdicated the government," &c.—makes this observation upon it : " The word *abdicated* relates to *all* the clauses aforegoing, as well as to his deserting the kingdom, or else they would have been wholly in vain." And that there might be no pretence for confining the *abdication* merely to the *withdrawing*, Lord Sommers farther observes, *that King James, by refusing to govern us according to that law by which he held the crown, implicitly renounced his title to it.*

If *Junius's* construction of the vote against Mr Walpole be now admitted (and indeed I cannot comprehend how it can honestly be disputed), the advocates of the House of Commons must either give up their precedent entirely, or be reduced to the necessity of maintaining one of the grossest absurdities imaginable, viz. " That a commitment to the Tower is a constituent part of, and contributes half at least to, the incapacitation of the person who suffers it."

I need not make you any excuse for endeavouring to keep alive the attention of the public to the decision of the Middlesex election. The more I consider it, the more I am convinced that, as a *fact*, it is indeed highly injurious to the rights of the people; but that, as a *precedent*, it is one of the most dangerous that ever was established against those who are to come after us. Yet I am so far a moderate man, that I verily believe the majority of the House of Commons, when they passed this dangerous vote, neither understood the question, nor knew the consequence of what they were doing. Their motives were rather despicable, than criminal, in the extreme. One effect they certainly did not foresee. They are now reduced to such a situation, that if a member of the present House of Commons were to conduct himself ever so improperly, and in reality deserve to be sent back to his constituents with a mark of disgrace, they would not dare to expel him ; because they know that the people, in order to try again the great question of right, or to thwart an odious House of Commons, would probably overlook his immediate unworthiness, and return the same person to Parliament.—But, in time, the precedent will gain strength. A future House of Commons will have no such apprehensions; consequently will not scruple to follow a precedent, which they did not establish. The miser himself seldom lives to enjoy the fruit of his extortion ; but his heir succeeds him of course, and takes possession without censure. No man expects him to make restitution ; and, no matter for his title, he lives quietly upon the estate.

PHILO JUNIUS.

I DO not mean to give an opinion upon the juſtice of the proceed-ings of the Houſe of Commons with regard to Mr. Walpole; but certainly, if I admitted their cenſure to be well founded, I could no way avoid agreeing with them in the conſequence they drew from it. I could never have a doubt, in law or reaſon, that a man con-victed of a high breach of truſt, and of a notorious corruption, in the execution of a public office, was and ought to be incapable of ſit-ting in the ſame parliament. Far from attempting to invalidate that vote, I ſhould have wiſhed that the incapacity declared by it could legally have been continued for ever.

Now, Sir, obſerve how forcibly the argument returns. The Houſe of Commons, upon the face of their proceedings, had the ſtrongeſt motives to declare Mr. Walpole incapable of being re-elected. They thought ſuch a man unworthy to ſit among them. To that point they proceeded, and no farther; for they reſpected the rights of the people, while they aſſerted their own. They did not infer from Mr. Walpole's incapacity that his opponent was duly elected; on the contrary, they declared Mr. Taylor " not duly elected," and the elec-tion itſelf void.

Such, however, is the precedent which my honeſt friend aſſures us is ſtrictly in point to prove, that expulſion of itſelf creates an in-capacity of being elected. If it had been ſo, the preſent Houſe of Commons ſhould at leaſt have followed ſtrictly the example before them, and ſhould have ſtated to us in the ſame vote the crimes for which they expelled Mr. Wilkes; whereas they reſolve ſimply, that, " having been expelled, he was and is incapable." In this proceed-ing I am authoriſed to affirm, they have neither ſtatute, nor cuſtom, nor reaſon, nor one ſingle precedent to ſupport them. On the other ſide, there is indeed a precedent ſo ſtrongly in point, that all the en-chanted caſtles of miniſterial magic fall before it. In the year 1698 (a period which the rankeſt Tory dare not except againſt), Mr. Wollafton was expelled, re-elected, and admitted to take his feat in the fame parliament. The miniftry have precluded themfelves from all objections drawn from the caufe of his expulfion; for they affirm abfolutely, that expulfion of itfelf creates the difability. Now, Sir, let fophiftry evade, let falfehood affert, and impudence deny—here ftands the precedent, a land-mark to direct us through a troubled fea of controverfy, confpicuous and unmoved.

I HAVE dwelt the longer upon the difcuffion of this point, becaufe, in *my* opinion, it comprehends the whole queftion. The reft is unworthy of notice. We are inquiring whether incapacity be or be not created by expulfion. In the cafes of Bedford and Malden, the incapacity of the perfons returned was matter of public notoriety, for it was created by act of parliament. But really, Sir, my honeft friend's fuppofitions are as unfavourable to him as his facts. He well knows that the clergy, befides that they are reprefented in common with their fellow-fubjects, have alfo a feparate parliament of their own: That their incapacity to fit in the Houfe of Commons has been confirmed by repeated decifions of the Houfe; and that the law of parliament declared by thofe decifions has been for above two centuries notorious and undifputed. The author is certainly at liberty to fancy cafes, and make whatever comparifons he thinks proper; his fuppofitions ftill continue as diftant from fact, as his wild difcourfes are from folid argument.

THE conclufion of his book is candid to extreme. He offers to grant me all I defire. He thinks he may fafely admit that the cafe of Mr. Walpole makes directly againft him, for it feems he has one grand folution *in petto* for all difficulties. *If* (fays he) *I were to allow all this, it will only prove, that the law of election was different in Queen Anne's time from what it is at prefent.*

THIS indeed is more than I expected. The principle, I know, has been maintained in fact; but I never expected to fee it fo formally declared. What can he mean? Does he affume this language to fatisfy the doubts of the people, or does he mean to roufe their indignation? Are the miniftry daring enough to affirm, that the Houfe of Commons have a right to make and unmake the law of parliament at their pleafure? Does the law of parliament, which we are fo often told is the law of the land,—does the common right of every fubject of the realm depend upon an arbitrary capricious vote of one branch of the legiflature?—The voice of truth and reafon muft be filent.

THE miniftry tell us plainly, that this is no longer a queftion of right, but of power and force alone. What was law yefterday is not law to-day;—and now it feems we have no better rule to live by, than the temporary difcretion and fluctuating integrity of the Houfe of Commons.

PROFESSIONS of patriotifm are become ftale and ridiculous. For my own part, I claim no merit from endeavouring to do a fervice to my fellow-fubjects. I have done it to the beft of my underftanding; and, without looking for the approbation of other men, my confcience is fatisfied. What remains to be done concerns the collective body of the people. They are now to determine for themfelves, whether they will firmly and conftitutionally affert their rights, or make an humble flavifh furrender of them at the feet of the miniftry. To a generous mind there cannot be a doubt. We owe it to our anceftors to preferve entire thefe rights which they have delivered to our care : We owe it to our pofterity not to fuffer their deareft inheritance to be deftroyed. But, if it were poffible for us to be infenfible of thefe facred claims, there is yet an obligation binding upon ourfelves, from which nothing can acquit us,—a perfonal intereft, which we cannot furrender. To alienate even our own rights would be a crime as much more enormous than fuicide, as a life of civil fecurity

and freedom is fuperior to a bare exiftence; and if life be the bounty of heaven, we fcornfully reject the nobleft part of the gift, if we
confent to furrender that certain rule of living, without which the
condition of human nature is not only miferable but contemptible.

JUNIUS.

LETTER XXI.

TO THE PRINTER OF THE PUBLIC ADVERTISER.

SIR,   *AUGUST* 22. 1769.

MUST beg of you to print a few lines in explanation of fome paffages in my laft letter, which I fee have been mifunderftood.

1. WHEN I faid that the Houfe of Commons never meant to found
Mr. Walpole's incapacity on his expulfion *only*, I meant no more
than to deny the general propofition, that expulfion *alone* creates the
incapacity. If there be any thing ambiguous in the expreffion, I beg
leave to explain it by faying, that, in my opinion, expulfion neither
creates, nor in any part contributes to create the incapacity in queftion.

2. I CAREFULLY avoided entering into the merits of Mr. Walpole's cafe. I did not inquire whether the Houfe of Commons acted
juftly, or whether they truly declared the law of parliament. My remarks went only to their apparent meaning and intention as it ftands
declared in their own refolution.

3. I NEVER meant to affirm, that a commitment to the Tower

created a difqualification. On the contrary, I confidered that idea as an abfurdity into which the miniftry muft inevitably fall, if they reafoned right upon their own principles.

THE cafe of Mr. Wollafton fpeaks for itfelf. The miniftry affert that *expulfion alone* creates an abfolute complete incapacity to be re-elected to fit in the fame parliament. This propofition they have uniformly maintained, without any condition or modification whatfoever. Mr. Wollafton was expelled, re-elected, and admitted to take his feat in the fame parliament.—I leave it to the public to determine, whether this be a plain matter of fact, or mere nonfenfe or declamation.

JUNIUS.

LETTER XXII.

TO THE PRINTER OF THE PUBLIC ADVERTISER.

SEPTEMBER 4. 1769.

ARGUMENT *againft* FACT, *or* A New Syftem of Political Logic, *by which the Miniftry have demonftrated, to the fatisfaction of their friends, that expulfion alone creates a complete incapacity to be re-elected;* alias, *that a fubject of this realm may be robbed of his common right by a vote of the Houfe of Commons.*

FIRST FACT.

Mr Wollafton in 1698 *was expelled, re-elected, and admitted to take his feat.*

ARGUMENT.

As this cannot conveniently be reconciled with our general pro-
P

pofition, it may be neceffary to fhift our ground, and look back to the *caufe* of Mr. Wollafton's expulfion. From thence it will appear clearly, that, " although he was expelled, he had not rendered him-felf a culprit too ignominious to fit in parliament ; and that, having refigned his employment, he was no longer incapacitated by law." *Vide Serious Confiderations*, p. 23. Or thus, "The Houfe, fomewhat *inaccurately*, ufed the word EXPELLED ; they fhould have called it AMOTION," *Vide Mungo's Cafe confidered*, p. 11. Or, in fhort, if thefe arguments fhould be thought infufficient, we may fairly deny the fact. For example—" I affirm that he was not re-elected. The fame Mr. Wollafton, who was expelled, was not again elected. The fame individual, if you pleafe, walked into the Houfe, and took his feat there ; but the fame perfon in law was not admitted a member of that parliament, from which he had been difcarded." *Vide Letter to Junius*, p. 12.

SECOND FACT.

Mr. Walpole having been committed to the Tower, and expelled for a high breach of truft and notorious corruption in a public office, was declared incapable, &c.

ARGUMENT.

FROM the terms of this vote, nothing can be more evident, than that the Houfe of Commons meant to fix the incapacity upon the punifhment, and not upon the crime ; but, left it fhould appear in a different light to weak uninformed perfons, it may be advifable to gut the refolution, and give it to the public, with all poffible folem-nity, in the following terms, viz. " Refolved, That Robert Walpole, Efq. having been that feffion of parliament expelled the Houfe, was and is incapable of being elected member to ferve in that prefent par-liament." *Vide Mungo on the ufe of quotations*, p. 11.

N.B. The author of the anfwer to Sir William Meredith feems to have made ufe of Mungo's quotation ; for in page 18, he affures us, " That the declaratory vote of the 17th of February 1769, was indeed a literal copy of the refolution of the Houfe in Mr. Walpole's cafe."

THIRD FACT.

His opponent, Mr. Taylor, having the fmalleft number of votes at the next election, was declared not duly elected.

ARGUMENT.

THIS fact we confider as directly in point to prove that Mr. Luttrell ought to be the fitting member, for the following reafons : " The burgeffes of Lynn could draw no other inference from this refolution but this, that, at a future election, and in cafe of a fimilar return, the Houfe would receive the fame candidate as duly elected, whom they had before rejected." *Vide Poftfcript to Junius,* p. 37. Or thus, " This their refolution leaves no room to doubt what part they *would* have taken, if, upon a fubfequent re-election of Mr. Walpole, there had been any other candidate in competition with him : For, by their vote, they could have no other intention than to admit fuch other candidate." *Vide Mungo's cafe confidered,* p. 39. Or take it in this light: The burgeffes of Lynn having, in defiance of the Houfe, retorted upon them a perfon whom they had branded with the moft ignominious marks of their difpleafure, were thereby fo well intitled to favour and indulgence, that the Houfe could do no lefs than rob Mr. Taylor of a right legally vefted in him, in order that the burgeffes might be apprifed of the law of parliament; which law the Houfe took a very direct way of explaining to them, by refolving that the candidate with the feweft votes was not duly elected : " And was not this much more equitable, more in the fpirit of that equal and fubftantial juftice which is the end of all law, than if they had violently adhered to the ftrict maxims of law ?" *Vide Serious Confiderations,* p. 33. and 34. " And if the prefent Houfe of Commons had chofen to follow the fpirit of this refolution, they would have received and eftablifhed the candidate with the feweft votes." *Vide Anfwer to Sir W. M.* p. 18.

PERMIT me now, Sir, to shew you, that the worthy Dr. Blackstone sometimes contradicts the miniftry as well as himself. The speech without doors afferts, p. 9. " That the legal effect of an incapacity, founded on a judicial determination of a complete court, is precisely the fame as that of an incapacity created by act of parliament."—Now for the doctor. *The law and the opinion of the judge are not always convertible terms, or one and the fame thing; fince it fometimes may happen that the judge may miftake the law.* Commentaries, vol. I. p. 71.

THE anfwer to Sir W. M. afferts, p. 23. " That the returning officer is not a judicial, but a purely minifterial officer. His return is no judicial act."—At 'em again, Doctor. *The Sheriff in his judicial capacity is to hear and determine caufes of forty fhillings value and under in his county court. He has alfo a judicial power in divers other civil caufes. He is likewife to decide the elections of knights of the fhire (fubject to the controul of the Houfe of Commons), to judge of the qualification of voters, and to return fuch as he fhall determine to be duly elected.* Vide Commentaries, vol. I. p. 332.

WHAT conclufion fhall we draw from fuch facts, and fuch arguments, fuch contradictions ? I cannot exprefs my opinion of the prefent miniftry more exactly than in the words of Sir Richard Steele: " That we are governed by a fet of drivellers, whofe folly takes away all dignity from diftrefs, and makes even calamity ridiculous."

PHILO JUNIUS.

LETTER XXIII.

TO HIS GRACE THE DUKE OF BEDFORD.

MY LORD,   *SEPTEMBER* 19. 1769.

YOU are fo little accuftomed to receive any marks of refpect or efteem from the public, that if, in the following lines, a compliment or expreffion of applaufe fhould efcape me, I fear you would confider it as a mockery of your eftablifhed character, and perhaps an infult to your underftanding. You have nice feelings, my Lord, if we may judge from your refentments. Cautious therefore of giving offence, where you have fo little deferved it, I fhall leave the illuftration of your virtues to other hands. Your friends have a privilege to play upon the eafinefs of your temper, or poffibly they are better acquainted with your good qualities than I am. You have done good by ftealth. The reft is upon record. You have ftill left ample room for fpeculation, when panegyric is exhaufted.

YOU are indeed a very confiderable man. The higheft rank; a fplendid fortune; and a name, glorious till it was yours—were fufficient to have fupported you with meaner abilities than I think you poffefs. From the firft, you derive a conftitutional claim to refpect; from the fecond, a natural extenfive authority; the laft created a partial expectation of hereditary virtues. The ufe you have made of thefe uncommon advantages might have been more honourable to yourfelf, but could not be more inftructive to mankind. We may trace it in the veneration of your country, the choice of your friends, and in the accomplifhment of every fanguine hope which the public might have conceived from the illuftrious name of Ruffel.

THE eminence of your ftation gave you a commanding profpect

of your duty. The road which led to honour was open to your view. You could not lofe it by miftake, and you had no temptation to depart from it by defign. Compare the natural dignity and importance of the richeft peer of England; the noble independence which he might have maintained in parliament, and the real intereft and refpect which he might have acquired, not only in parliament, but through the whole kingdom: Compare thefe glorious diftinctions with the ambition of holding a fhare in government, the emoluments of a place, the fale of a borough, or the purchafe of a corporation; and though you may not regret the virtues which create refpect, you may fee with anguifh how much real importance and authority you have loft. Confider the character of an independent virtuous Duke of Bedford; imagine what he might be in this country, then reflect one moment upon what you are. If it be poffible for me to withdraw my attention from the fact, I will tell you in the theory what fuch a man might be.

CONSCIOUS of his own weight and importance, his conduct in parliament would be directed by nothing but the conftitutional duty of a peer. He would confider himfelf as a guardian of the laws. Willing to fupport the juft meafures of government, but determined to obferve the conduct of the minifter with fufpicion, he would oppofe the violence of faction with as much firmnefs as the incroachments of prerogative. He would be as little capable of bargaining with the minifter for places for himfelf or his dependents, as of defcending to mix himfelf in the intrigues of oppofition. Whenever an important queftion called for his opinion in parliament, he would be heard by the moft profligate minifter with deference and refpect. His authority would either fanctify or difgrace the meafures of government. The people would look up to him as their protector; and a virtuous prince would have one honeft man in his dominions, in whofe integrity and judgment he might fafely confide. If it fhould be the will of Providence to afflict him with a domeftic misfortune,

he would fubmit to the ftroke with feeling, but not without dignity *. He would confider the people as his children, and receive a
generous heart-felt confolation in the fympathifing tears and bleffings
of his country.

YOUR Grace may probably difcover fomething more intelligible
in the negative part of this illuftrious character. The man I have defcribed would never proftitute his dignity in parliament by an indecent violence either in oppofing or defending a minifter. He would
not at one moment rancoroufly perfecute, at another bafely cringe to
the favourite of his Sovereign. After outraging the royal dignity with
peremptory conditions little fhort of menace and hoftility, he would
never defcend to the humility of foliciting an interview § with the
favourite, and of offering to recover at any price the honour of his
friendfhip. Though deceived perhaps in his youth, he would not,
through the courfe of a long life, have invariably chofen his friends
from among the moft profligate of mankind. His own honour would
have forbidden him from mixing his private pleafures or converfa-
tion with jockies, gamefters, blafphemers, gladiators, or buffoons.—
He would then have never felt, much lefs would he have fubmitted
to, the difhoneft neceffity of engaging in the interefts and intrigues
of his dependents; of fupplying their vices, or relieving their beggary, at the expence of his country. He would not have betrayed
fuch ignorance or fuch contempt of the conftitution, as openly to
avow, in a court of juftice, the purchafe and fale of a borough ||.—
He would not have thought it confiftent with his rank in the ftate,
or even with his perfonal importance, to be the little tyrant of a

---

* The Duke lately loft his only fon by a fall from his horfe.

§ At this interview, which paffed at the houfe of the late Lord Eglintoun, Lord Bute told the Duke
that he was determined never to have any connexion with a man who had fo bafely betrayed him.

|| In an anfwer in Chancery, in a fuit againft him to recover a large fum paid him by a perfon whom
he had undertaken to return to parliament for one of his Grace's boroughs. He was compelled to repay
the money.

little corporation *. He would never have been infulted with virtues which he had laboured to extinguifh ; nor fuffered the difgrace
of a mortifying defeat, which has made him ridiculous and contemptible, even to the few by whom he was not detefted. I reve-
rence the afflictions of a good man—his forrows are facred. But
how can we take part in the diftrefles of a man whom we can neither love nor efteem, or feel for a calamity, of which he himfelf is
infenfible? Where was the father's heart, when he could look for,
or find, an immediate confolation for the lofs of an only fon, in con-
fultations and bargains for a place at court, and even in the mifery
of ballotting at the India-houfe!

ADMITTING then that you have miftaken or deferted thofe honourable principles which ought to have directed your conduct—
admitting that you have as little claim to private affection as to public efteem—let us fee with what abilities, with what degree of judgment, you have carried your own fyftem into execution. A great
man, in the fuccefs, and even in the magnitude of his crimes, finds a
refcue from contempt. Your Grace is every way unfortunate. Yet
I will not look back to thofe ridiculous fcenes, by which, in your
earlier days, you thought it an honour to be diftinguifhed § ; the recorded ftripes, the public infamy, your own fufferings, or Mr Rig-
by's fortitude. Thefe events undoubtedly left an impreffion, though
not upon your mind. To fuch a mind it may perhaps be a pleafure
to reflect, that there is hardly a corner of any of his Majefty's king-

---

* Of Bedford ; where the tyrant was held in fuch contempt and deteftation, that, in order to deliver
themfelves from him, they admitted a great number of ftrangers to the freedom. To make his defeat
truly ridiculous, he tried his whole ftrength againft Mr. *Horne*, and was beaten upon his own ground.

§ Mr. Hefton Humphrey, a country attorney, horfewhipped the Duke, with equal juftice, feverity, and
perfeverance, on the courfe at Litchfield. *Rigby* and Lord *Trentham* were alfo cudgelled in a moft exem-
plary manner. This gave rife to the following ftory : " When the late King heard that Sir Edward Hawke
had given the French a *drubbing*, his Majefty, who had never received that kind of chaftifement, was pleafed to afk Lord Chefterfield the meaning of the word.—Sir (fays Lord Chefterfield), the meaning of the
word—but here comes the Duke of Bedford, who is better able to explain it to your Majefty than I
am."

doms, except France, in which, at one time or another, your valuable life has not been in danger. Amiable man! we fee and acknowledge the protection of Providence, by which you have fo often efcaped the perfonal deteftation of your fellow-fubjects, and are ftill referved for the public juftice of your country.

Your hiftory begins to be important at that aufpicious period at which you were deputed to reprefent the Earl of Bute at the Court of Verfailles. It was an honourable office, and executed with the fame fpirit with which it was accepted. Your patrons wanted an ambaffador, who would fubmit to make conceffions, without daring to infift upon any honourable condition for his Sovereign. Their bufinefs required a man who had as little feeling for his own dignity as for the welfare of his country; and they found him in the firft rank of the nobility. Belleifle, Goree, Guadaloupe, St. Lucia, Martinique, the Fifhery, and the Havannah, are glorious monuments of your Grace's talents for negotiation. My Lord, we are too well acquainted with your pecuniary character to think it poffible that fo many public facrifices fhould have been made, without fome private compenfations. Your conduct carries with it an internal evidence, beyond all the legal proofs of a court of juftice. Even the callous pride of Lord Egremont was alarmed *. He faw and felt his own difhonour in correfponding with you; and there certainly was a moment at which he meant to have refifted, had not a fatal lethargy prevailed over his faculties, and carried all fenfe and memory away with it.

I will not pretend to fpecify the fecret terms on which you were invited to fupport an § adminiftration which Lord Bute pretended

---

* This man, notwithftanding his pride and Tory principles, had fome Englifh ftuff in him. Upon an official letter he wrote to the Duke of Bedford, the Duke defired to be recalled, and it was with the utmoft difficulty that Lord Bute could appeafe him.

§ Mr. Grenville, Lord Halifax, and Lord Egremont.

Q

to leave in full poffeffion of their minifterial authority, and perfectly mafters of themfelves. He was not of a temper to relinquifh power, though he retired from employment. Stipulations were certainly made between your Grace and him, and certainly violated. After two years fubmiffion, you thought you had collected a ftrength fufficient to controul his influence, and that it was your turn to be a tyrant, becaufe you had been a flave. When you found yourfelf miftaken in your opinion of your gracious mafter's firmnefs, difappointment got the better of all your humble difcretion, and carried you to an excefs of outrage to his perfon, as diftant from true fpirit as from all decency and refpect *. After robbing him of the rights of a King, you would not permit him to preferve the honour of a gentleman. It was then Lord Weymouth was nominated to Ireland, and difpatched (we well remember with what indecent hurry) to plunder the treafury of the firft fruits of an employment which you well know he was never to execute §.

THIS fudden declaration of war againft the favourite might have given you a momentary merit with the public, if it had either been adopted upon principle, or maintained with refolution. Without looking back to all your former fervility, we need only obferve your fubfequent conduct, to fee upon what motives you acted. Apparently united with Mr. Grenville, you waited until Lord Rockingham's feeble adminiftration fhould diffolve in its own weaknefs. The moment their difmiffion was fufpected, the moment you perceived that another fyftem was adopted in the clofet, you thought it no difgrace to return to your former dependence, and folicit once more the

---

* The miniftry having endeavoured to exclude the Dowager out of the regency bill, the Earl of Bute determined to difmifs them. Upon this the Duke of Bedford demanded an audience of the ——; reproached him in plain terms with his duplicity, bafenefs, falfehood, treachery, and hypocrify—repeatedly gave him the lie, and left him in convulfions.

§ He received three thoufand pounds for plate and equipage money.

friendfhip of Lord Bute. You begged an interview, at which he
had fpirit enough to treat you with contempt.

IT would be now of little ufe to point out, by what a train of
weak injudicious meafures it became neceffary, or was thought fo,
to call you back to a fhare in the adminiftration *. The friends,
whom you did not in the laft inftance defert, were not of a character to add ftrength or credit to government; and at that time your
alliance with the Duke of Graftoh was, I prefume, hardly forefeen.
We muft look for other ftipulations, to account for that fudden refolution of the clofet, by which three of your dependents § (whofe
charaɗers, I think, cannot be lefs refpeɗed than they are) were ad-
vanced to offices, through which you might again controul the minifter, and probably engrofs the whole direɗion of affairs.

THE poffeffion of abfolute power is now once more within your
reach. The meafures you have taken to obtain and confirm it are
too grofs to efcape the eyes of a difcerning judicious prince. His
palace is befieged; the lines of circumvallation are drawing round
him; and unlefs he finds a refource in his own aɗivity, or in the
attachment of the real friends of his family, the beft of princes muft
fubmit to the confinement of a ftate-prifoner, until your Grace's
death, or fome lefs fortunate event, fhall raife the fiege. For the
prefent, you may fafely refume that ftyle of infult and menace, which
even a private gentleman cannot fubmit to hear without being contemptible. Mr. Mackenzie's hiftory is not yet forgotten; and you
may find precedents enough of the mode in which an imperious
fubjeɗ may fignify his pleafure to his Sovereign. Where will this
gracious Monarch look for affiftance, when the wretched Grafton

---

* When Earl.Gower was appointed Prefident of the Council, the King with his ufual fincerity affured
him, that he had not had one happy moment fince the Duke of Bedford left him.

§ Lords Gower, Weymouth, and Sandwich.

could forget his obligations to his mafter, and defert him for a hollow alliance with *fuch* a man as the Duke of Bedford !

LET us confider you then as arrived at the fummit of worldly greatnefs : Let us fuppofe, that all your plans of avarice and ambition are accomplifhed, and your moft fanguine wifhes gratified in the fear as well as the hatred of the people : Can age itfelf forget that you are in the laft act of life ? Can grey hairs make folly venerable ? and is there no period to be referved for meditation and retirement ? For fhame, my Lord ! Let it not be recorded of you, that the lateft moments of your life were dedicated to the fame unworthy purfuits, the fame bufy agitations, in which your youth and manhood were exhaufted. Confider, that, although you cannot difgrace your former life, you are violating the character of age, and expofing the impotent imbecillity after you have loft the vigour of the paffions.

YOUR friends will afk, perhaps, Whither fhall this unhappy old man retire ? Can he remain in the metropolis, where his life has been fo often threatened, and his palace fo often attacked ? If he returns to Wooburn, fcorn and mockery await him. He muft create a folitude round his eftate, if he would avoid the face of reproach and derifion. At Plymouth, his deftruction would be more than probable ; at Exeter, inevitable. No honeft Englifhman will ever forget his attachment, nor any honeft Scotchman forgive his treachery, to Lord Bute. At every town he enters, he muft change his liveries and name. Whichever way he flies the *hue and cry* of the country purfues him.

IN another kingdom, indeed, the bleffings of his adminiftration have been more fenfibly felt ; his virtues better underftood ; or at worft they will not, for him alone, forget their hofpitality. As well might VERRES have returned to Sicily. You have twice efcaped, my Lord; beware of a third experiment. The indignation of a whole people, plundered, infulted, and oppreffed as they have been, will not always be difappointed.

It is in vain therefore to fhift the fcene. You can no more fly from your enemies than from yourfelf. Perfecuted abroad, you look into your own heart for confolation, and find nothing but reproaches and defpair. But, my Lord, you may quit the field of bufinefs, though not the field of danger; and though you cannot be fafe, you may ceafe to be ridiculous. I fear you have liftened too long to the advice of thofe pernicious friends, with whofe interefts you have fordidly united your own, and for whom you have facrificed every thing that ought to be dear to a man of honour. They are ftill bafe enough to encourage the follies of your age, as they once did the vices of your youth. As little acquainted with the rules of decorum as with the laws of morality, they will not fuffer you to profit by experience, nor even to confult the propriety of a bad character.— Even now they tell you, that life is no more than a dramatic fcene, in which the hero fhould preferve his confiftency to the laft; and that as you lived without virtue, you fhould die without repentance..

JUNIUS..

LETTER XXIV.

TO JUNIUS..

SIR, *SEPTEMBER* 14. 1769.

HAVING accidentally feen a *republication* of your letters, wherein you have been pleafed to *affert*, that I had *fold* the companions of my fuccefs, I am again obliged to declare the faid affertion to be a

moſt *infamous* and *malicious falſehood;* and I *again* call upon you to
ſtand forth, avow yourſelf, and *prove* the charge. If you can make
it out to the ſatisfaction of any one man in the kingdom, I will be
content to be thought the worſt man in it ; if you do not, what muſt
the nation think of you ? *Party* has nothing to do in this affair : You
have made a perſonal attack upon my honour, defamed me by a
moſt vile calumny, which might poſſibly have ſunk into oblivion,
had not ſuch uncommon pains been taken to renew and perpetuate
this ſcandal, chiefly becauſe it has been told in good language : For
I give you full credit for your elegant diction, well-turned periods,
and Attic wit : But wit is oftentimes falſe, though it may appear
brilliant ; which is exactly the caſe of your *whole performance.* But,
Sir, I am obliged in the moſt *ſerious* manner to accuſe you of being
guilty of *falſities.* You have ſaid the thing that is *not.* To ſupport
your ſtory, you have recourſe to the following *irreſiſtible* argument :
" You *ſold* the companions of your victory, becauſe when the 16th
regiment was given to *you,* you was *ſilent.* The concluſion is inevitable."—I believe that ſuch *deep* and *acute reaſoning* could only come
from ſuch an extraordinary writer as *Junius.* But unfortunately for
you, the *premiſes* as well as the *concluſion* are abſolutely *falſe.* Many
applications have been made to the miniſtry on the ſubject of the
Manilla ranſom *ſince* the time of my being colonel of that regiment.
As I have for ſome years quitted London, I was obliged to have recourſe to the Honourable Colonel Monſon and Sir Samuel Corniſh
to *negotiate* for me ; in the laſt autumn, I perſonally delivered a memorial to the Earl of Shelburn at his ſeat in Wiltſhire. As you have
told us of your importance, that you are a perſon of *rank* and *fortune,*
and above a *common* bribe, you may in all probability be not *unknown*
to his Lordſhip, who can ſatisfy you of the truth of what I ſay. But
I ſhall now take the liberty, Sir, to ſeize your battery, and turn
it againſt yourſelf. If your puerile and tinſel logic could carry
the leaſt weight or conviction with it, how muſt you ſtand affected
by the *inevitable concluſion,* as you are pleaſed to term it ? According

to *Junius*, *Silence* is *guilt*. In many of the public papers, you have been called in the moſt direct and offenſive terms a *liar* and a *coward*. When did you reply to theſe foul accuſations? You have been quite *ſilent*; quite chop-fallen: Therefore, *becauſe* you was *ſilent*, the nation has a right to pronounce you to be both a liar and a coward from your own argument. But, Sir, I will give you fair play; I will afford you an opportunity to wipe off the firſt appellation, by deſiring the proofs of your charge againſt me. Produce them! To wipe off the laſt, produce *yourſelf*. People cannot bear any longer your *lion's ſkin*, and the deſpicable *impoſture* of the *old Roman name* which you have *affected*. For the future aſſume the name of ſome *modern* bravo and dark aſſaſſin *: Let your appellation have ſome affinity to your practice. But if I muſt *periſh*, *Junius*, let me *periſh* in the face of day; be for *once* a generous and open enemy. I allow that Gothic *appeals* to cold iron are no better proofs of a man's honeſty and veracity, than hot iron and burning ploughſhares are of *female chaſtity*; but a ſoldier's honour is as delicate as a woman's; it muſt not be ſuſpected; you have dared to throw more than a ſuſpicion upon mine: You cannot but know the conſequences, which even the meekneſs of Chriſtianity would pardon me for, after the injury you have done me.

WILLIAM DRAPER.

---

* Was *Brutus* an *ancient* bravo and dark aſſaſſin? or does Sir W. D. think it criminal to ſtab a tyrant to the heart?

LETTER XXV.

Hæret lateri lethalis arundo.

......•......

TO SIR WILLIAM DRAPER, K. B.

SIR, *SEPTEMBER* 25. 1769.

AFTER fo long an interval, I did not expect to fee the debate revived between us. My anfwer to your laft letter fhall be fhort ; for I write to you with reluctance, and I hope we fhall now conclude our correfpondence for ever.

HAD you been originally and without provocation attacked by an anonymous writer, you would have fome right to demand his name. But in this caufe you are a volunteer. You engaged in it with the unpremeditated gallantry of a foldier. You were content to fet your name in oppofition to a man who would probably continue in concealment. You underftood the terms upon which we were to correfpond, and gave at leaft a tacit affent to them. After voluntarily attacking me under the character of Junius, what poffible right have you to know me under any other ? Will you forgive me if I infinuate to you, that you forefaw fome honour in the apparent fpirit of coming forward in perfon, and that you were not quite indifferent to the difplay of your literary qualifications ?

YOU cannot but know, that the republication of my letters was no more than a catchpenny contrivance of a printer, in which it was impoffible I fhould be concerned, and for which I am no way anfwerable. At the fame time I wifh you to underftand, that, if I do not take the trouble of reprinting thefe papers, it is not from any fear of giving offence to Sir William Draper.

YOUR remarks upon a fignature adopted merely for diftinction are unworthy of notice ; but when you tell me I have fubmitted to be called a liar and a coward, I muft afk you in my turn, whether you think ferioufly it any way incumbent on me to take notice of the filly invectives of every fimpleton who writes in a newfpaper ; and what opinion you would have conceived of my difcretion, if I had fuffered myfelf to be the dupe of fo fhallow an artifice ?

YOUR appeal to the fword, though confiftent enough with your late profeffion, will neither prove your innocence nor clear you from fufpicion.—Your complaints with regard to the Manilla ranfom were for a confiderable time a diftrefs to government. You were appointed (greatly out of your turn) to the command of a regiment, and *during that adminiftration* we heard no more of Sir William Draper. The facts of which I fpeak may indeed be varioufly accounted for, but they are too notorious to be denied ; and I think you might have learnt at the univerfity, that a falfe conclufion is an error in argument, not a breach of veracity. Your folicitations, I doubt not, were renewed under *another* adminiftration. Admitting the fact, I fear an indifferent perfon would only infer from it, that experience had made you acquainted with the benefits of complaining. Remember, Sir, that you have yourfelf confeffed, that, *confidering the critical fituation of this country, the miniftry are in the right to temporife with Spain.* This confeffion reduces you to an unfortunate dilemma. By renewing your folicitations, you muft either mean to force your country into a war at a moft unfeafonable juncture ; or, having no view or expectation of that kind, that you look for nothing but a private compenfation to yourfelf.

As to me, it is by no means neceffary that I fhould be expofed to the refentment of the worft and the moft powerful men in this country, though I may be indifferent about yours. Though *you* would fight, there are others who would affaffinate.

R.